Above: Beef Balls in Barbecue Sauce (page 26); Below: Roast Beef with Pecan Sauce (page 26)

BRILLIANT BARBECUES

Written & Compiled by
Reuben Solomon

Photography
Ray Joyce

Illustrations
Barbara Rodanska &
Bruce Whatley

MURDOCH BOOKS
Sydney • London • Vancouver

Barbecue Brilliance

It all began when prehistoric man created fire from two pieces of wood. Starting a fire wasn't that bad, he thought, it certainly gave him a warm glow. So why not try using it to enhance the flavour of that lousy dinosaur chop he was saving for his dinner. It must have tasted good, because centuries later man is still cooking his meals on an outdoor fire, sometimes burning it beyond recognition and having one heck of a good time in the process.

Over the years I've travelled to many countries which have their own unique style of outdoor cooking. In the Pacific Islands, hungry tourists gather to enjoy the classic Luau. Here, huge long pits are half filled with white-hot rocks and layered with meat, fish and yams wrapped in leaves. The foods are then covered and left to cook until tender. When retrieved from the earth oven, they are unwrapped and served without delay. Singapore, Malaysia and Indonesia have modest road-side stalls where tasty spiced satays are served over coals fanned with a palm frond to generate heat. In the same countries, exclusive hotels encourage you to cook your own over a mini-barbecue placed on your table. In Kashmir, wayside stalls feature charcoal-fired tandoor ovens. Skewered lamb and yeasty naan bread are cooked to order in minutes because of the intense heat of the tandoor.

With a minimum of effort, the recipes in **Brilliant Barbecues** allow you to explore a world of flavour. Feel free to improvise, using the ingredients that you prefer. Most of the ingredients used throughout the book are readily available in supermarkets, delicatessens or good food outlets.

There are some practical tips to save your sanity during the hour or so before the barbecue meal is ready and you can feel your guests becoming restless. Be ready. Have dips, chips, nibbles on hand – anything to keep them munching and crunching and take the pressure off. Not much you can do if a cool southerly is blowing and dissipating most of the heat from your glowing coals. This is what makes it so difficult to give an exact cooking time ... barbecues are subject to circumstances beyond our control. The variables are many.

Some recipes should be cooked before the hungry hordes descend. This allows you more space on the barbecue to cook the main course. Most appetisers, dips, vegetables, salads and desserts can be made in advance and are as important as the main dish itself.

If you are barbecuing with family or friends, I am sure you will find, among my barbecue recipes, something that just hits the spot.

Reuben Solomon

REUBEN SOLOMON

Front cover – Above: Beef Teriyaki with Onion Rings (page 25)
Below: Chilli Scallops and Prawn Kebabs (page 64)
Back cover – Left: Roast Beef with Pecan Sauce (page 26)
Right: Beef Balls in Barbecue Sauce (page 26)

CONTENTS

FOR YOUR CONVENIENCE WE HAVE USED THE FOLLOWING
COOKERY RATINGS TO GRADE EACH RECIPE

COOKERY RATING

easy   a little care needed   for confident cooks

SELECTING A BARBECUE

Bigger is not necessarily better. The joy of barbecuing is that it is not dependent on expensive, state of the art equipment. While there are advantages in owning a barbecue that lights instantly and offers the option of covered cooking, it is quite possible to cook successfully on something much more basic. Your barbecue needn't be a major investment. If you have a few spare bricks lying about, all you need to buy is a steel grill and, voilà! – a barbecue.

OWNER / BUILDER MODELS

If you're building your own, three-sided is preferable, to give some protection from wind. If you want to take the basic brick model upmarket, add a rack a couple of centimetres off the ground and place your fuel on that. Now that the air can circulate, your fire will burn even better. Most things can be cooked successfully on this simple contraption.

The only setback is that with grill alone you're limited to cooking pieces of food large enough that they won't fall between the bars. If you don't have a flat plate, a cast iron pan can broaden your culinary repertoire to include things such as onion rings, prawns, scallops and hamburgers.

HIBACHI

This barbecue has been around for a long time and is unbeatable for portability. Features include adjustable racks (closer or farther from the heat source) and air-vented fire bowls with grates that allow for greater heat control.

Read the manufacturers' recommendation for preferred fuel. The lid acts like an oven, making it possible to cook large joints of meat and whole poultry. It also enables you to smoke food, with the addition of special woods such as mesquite or hickory.

GAS BARBECUES

These vary in design. Basic gas barbecues offer grill cooking, while features such as flat plate, rotisserie and hood are optional – available in the top of the range models. Choose the one that best suits your needs, with electronic ignition if that's an option. Volcanic rock means you'll never need fuel, but you can try charcoal or briquets for a change. A layer of volcanic rocks placed over the gas burners gets glowing hot, but if you replace it with charcoal or briquets, you get more of that 'over the coals' flavour. Add a few water-soaked wood chips (woods such as hickory or mesquite) and you have the best of both worlds – ease and speed of getting the barbecue going, and the fragrance of a wood fire. Some barbecues have adjustable racks to compensate and regulate the intensity of heat by putting more or less distance between embers and food. However, with gas barbecues using volcanic rocks, the heat is regulated at each burner. There are gas barbecues fitted with a hood which are very useful for roasting, and some with a special ring to hold a wok situated at one end. The wok is excellent for stir-fry dishes, fried rice or noodles, while allowing you to continue using the rest of the barbecue for traditional grilling.

BARBECUE BASICS

Fuel to the fire. It is probably possible to light a barbecue by rubbing two sticks together. I once managed it as a boy scout, but since matches are both affordable and ubiquitous I don't think I could, in fairness, keep the guests waiting while I tried to repeat that feat.

If you're not good at building fires, there is no shame (but a lot of sense) in using a few fire starters to keep the home fires burning. They're mandatory with coal and briquets, which would be almost impossible to light with matches alone. Don't be put off by the pungent smell. It takes 20 minutes to get coals glowing and even longer for heat beads. By then the fire starters have served their purpose and are quite odourless. When briquets (made of compressed coal dust) and charcoal are well alight the flames will die down and a grey ash will appear all over the red-hot glowing coals.

A good way to find out if the heat is right is to hold the palm of your hand about 10 cm (4 inches) above the glowing coals. If you pull it away within two seconds, you know the barbecue is ready for the food. Likewise, when cooking over a wood fire, make certain that the flames have died down completely to leave glowing coals, covered with ash, before starting to cook. The flavour is unique. Some leaves and twigs from certain trees, especially anything with a milky white sap are not suitable to use on the barbecue so, if in doubt, leave it out. If you'd rather collect than buy wood, just be sure that what you're gathering isn't going to make your family barbie front page news!

Smoke flavour can be achieved on even the humblest barbecue with the addition of water-soaked mesquite or hickory chips just prior to cooking. However, to smoke-cook foods the indirect way, you will need to use some kind of covered barbecue. This method needs a drip pan (a baking dish will do) containing 4 cups of water to be positioned beneath food for smoking.

1 Put soaked wood chips in a small loaf tin, or make an open-ended roll out of doubled foil, punching some holes in the top to allow smoke to escape evenly.

2 Place to the side of food to be cooked. With indirect cooking on a gas barbecue, keep the burner lit under the wood chips and turn off the burner that's under the food. It's a slow-cooking method, but the smoke flavour will be much stronger than in direct smoke-cooked foods.

If cooking whole joints, check for 'doneness' with a meat thermometer or, in the case of poultry, by inserting a metal skewer in the thigh and making sure that the juices that run out are clear. If the juices are pink, longer cooking time is needed.

If using a kettle barbecue, arrange the coals so that they are to the sides of the drip pan and place wood chips over coals. Place food to be smoked on a grill or wire rack over the drip pan, but not touching the water. The steam helps to keep the food moist.

EQUIPMENT and ACCESSORIES

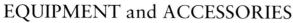

If you know an avid barbecue chef, you'll never be stuck for ideas when it comes to birthday and Christmas gifts. Don't be intimidated by the list of utensils; you can make a good start with even the first half dozen.

● A stiff wire brush/scraper – for brushing and scraping away burnt-on food from grill bars and flat plate.

● Gas lighter – a must for gas barbecues without automatic lighter.

● Long-handled tongs – for turning and moving food and coals while cooking and helps to prevent singed hands and arms.

● Metal frying slice – good for lifting hamburgers, onion rings, fried eggs, fish fillets etc.

● Long, sharp knife – for carving large pieces of meat or poultry.

● Heatproof mitts – especially for handling skewers and cast iron pans.

● Water spray – to subdue flare-ups.

● A fire blanket – keep one on hand wherever you cook.

● Skewers – long and flat metal are preferable, although bamboo works well if thoroughly soaked in water before use.

● Bristle basting brush or bulb baster – for coating with sauce or marinade.

● Wire fish frame – to hold fish together as it cooks and for easy turning.

● Rotisserie – for cooking large joints of meat evenly.

● Meat thermometer – to test large cuts of meat for doneness.

● Non-stick baking paper and heavy duty foil – non-stick baking paper is an ideal cooking medium, perfect for roasting and baking. I prefer not to cook directly in foil; sweet things are more prone to sticking or burning, while acid marinades can react with the aluminium.

Irresistible Appetisers

SPEND A LITTLE time planning your appetisers and your barbecue will get off to a good start. Crusty French bread or Italian breadsticks served with tasty dips and spreads are sure winners. So, too, is Guacamole served with crisp corn chips, or Nachos or try offering triangles of flat bread with Simple Eggplant Dip for a Middle Eastern touch.

Most importantly, your appetisers should leave your guests with plenty of room for the main event, so don't make too many or too much – just enough to stop them breathing down your neck while waiting ... and it will be worth waiting for.

Clockwise from top: Nachos (page 12), Bacon with Oysters and Prunes and Red Caviar Dip (page 13)

Guacamole

You'll love the taste and buttery texture of this dip. Serve, within a couple of hours of making, at room temperature.

PREPARATION TIME: *10 minutes*
COOKING TIME: *Nil*
SERVES 4-6

1 large ripe avocado
1 small tomato, seeded and
finely chopped
2 tablespoons finely chopped Spanish
onion or 3 spring onions
2 teaspoons olive oil
1 clove garlic, crushed
salt and pepper, to taste
1 tablespoon lime juice (see Note)

Peel and mash the avocado. Mix in the other ingredients and adjust seasoning. Serve with toasted corn chips.
Note: For that extra kick to the taste buds, sprinkle liberally with Tabasco or chilli sauce. If limes are scarce, replace with lemon juice.

Lemon, lime and Bitters is a quick and easy refreshing drink. Sprinkle the inside of tall glasses with three or four drops of Angostura aromatic bitters. Add crushed ice, a little lime juice cordial and a slice of lemon. Top with lemon squash or lemonade. Serve immediately.

Guacamole

Nachos

This popular recipe can be made as a one-dish meal when prepared in quantity. Make sure you have lots of cold drinks around to 'put out the fire'.

PREPARATION TIME: *10 minutes*
COOKING TIME: *25 minutes*
SERVES 6-8

¼ cup oil
1 large onion, finely chopped
2 cloves garlic, crushed
2 large ripe tomatoes, chopped
¼ cup tomato paste
2 canned jalapeno chillies (see Note)
1 x 465 g can red kidney beans
Tabasco sauce, to taste
2 x 375 g packets of corn chips
2½ cups grated Cheddar cheese

1 Heat oil in a medium pan or wok and cook onions until soft and golden. Add garlic, chopped tomatoes and tomato paste. Cook until tomatoes are soft.
2 Chop chillies. Rinse, drain and mash red kidney beans. Add to the cooked onions, garlic and tomato. Cook a further 5 minutes, stirring occasionally. Season to taste with Tabasco sauce, remove from the heat.
3 Arrange one packet corn chips in a flat heatproof tray. Spoon over half the kidney bean mixture and top with 1 cup grated cheese. Repeat with remaining ingredients to make a second layer.
4 Preheat the kettle barbecue. Place the nachos on a rack and cook with the hood down over a moderate heat until cheese is bubbly and melted. If cooking on an open barbecue, cover with a double layer of foil and cook on the flat plate for 10-12 minutes or until cheese is melted and bubbly.
Note: Canned jalapeno chillies are available from some delicatessens and wherever Mexican ingredients are sold. If jalapeno chillies are unavailable use one small fresh chilli, finely chopped. Nachos can also be cooked in a moderate oven 180°C for about 12 minutes or until they are hot. Serve immediately.

Bacon with Oysters and Prunes

Cook these savouries on the outer edge of the barbecue to prevent over-cooking.

PREPARATION TIME: *10 minutes*
COOKING TIME: *6 minutes*
SERVES 8

12 soft prunes
12 rashers of bacon
12 oysters, on the shell or bottled
Worcestershire sauce
ground black pepper, to taste
Tabasco sauce, to taste

1 Pit prunes. Trim the rind from the bacon and cut each rasher into two pieces. Wrap a portion of bacon around each prune and secure with bamboo skewers.
2 Remove the oysters from the half shell or drain from the liquid if required. Sprinkle lightly with Worcestershire sauce and pepper. Wrap each oyster in bacon, securing with a skewer as before.
3 Lightly oil the outer edge of a preheated barbecue flat plate. Cook the savouries until bacon is crisp. Serve warm, with a dash of Tabasco sauce.

Red Caviar Dip

If your sour cream is a little on the thin side, omit the lemon juice.

PREPARATION TIME: *10 minutes*
COOKING TIME: *Nil*
SERVES 6

1 x 50 g jar red lumpfish caviar
1 cup sour cream
3 spring onions, finely chopped
ground black pepper, to taste
2 teaspoons lime or lemon juice

1 Set aside about a teaspoon of caviar for garnish. In a bowl mix together all the ingredients, seasoning with ground pepper to taste.
2 Stir in lemon juice. Garnish with the reserved caviar.

Simple Eggplant Dip

This popular Lebanese dip is also known as *Baba Ganoush*. Although the best flavour comes when eggplants are cooked over coals, don't try to start this dip while your guests are present – it is one of those items that should be made and ready.

PREPARATION TIME: *10 minutes*
COOKING TIME: *30 minutes*
SERVES 4

4 medium eggplants
3 tablespoons olive oil
1 clove garlic, crushed
1 teaspoon ground oregano
1 small onion, finely chopped
½ teaspoon ground black pepper
1 tablespoon lime or lemon juice
salt, to taste
flat-leaved parsley, to garnish

1 Place the eggplant on barbecue grill and cook over high heat, turn the eggplant with tongs until all sides are blackened and it feels soft when gently prodded. This takes about 30 minutes.
2 Plunge eggplants in bowl of ice water. Drain on absorbent paper and peel away outer skin and discard.
3 Mash the flesh using a potato masher or food processor, add the olive oil, garlic, oregano and onion. Season to taste with ground pepper, lime juice and salt. Garnish with flat-leaved parsley. Serve with Middle Eastern bread or Crispy Lavash Triangles.
Note: Eggplants may also be cooked under a conventional hot grill.

Crispy Lavash Triangles
Combine
1 tablespoon each of ground dried cumin and ground dried oregano with
1 teaspoon each of ground pepper, ground sweet paprika and
2 teaspoons each of garlic powder and salt. Brush four pieces lavash bread lightly with olive oil on one side. Sprinkle sparingly with combined spices. Cut bread into oblong pieces and place on a tray. Place tray on the barbecue and heat until crisp. Or bake in a preheated moderate oven 180°C until crisp. Serve with dips or as a snack with drinks.

Simple Eggplant Dip

Barbecued Octopus

Octopus can be cooked by two different methods. In some recipes it is cooked for a long period of time, which in fact cooks it until tender, toughens it and then tenderises it again during the extended cooking time. The alternative method cooks the octopus for only a very short time until tender, making this an ideal method for the barbecue.

PREPARATION TIME: *20 minutes +*
1 hour marinating
COOKING TIME: *2 minutes*
SERVES 6-8

1 kg baby octopus

MARINADE
2 cloves garlic, crushed
2 tablespoons olive oil
2 tablespoons lime or lemon juice
½ teaspoon ground black pepper
1-2 teaspoons liquid smoke
(optional, see Note)
1 teaspoon hot chilli sauce
salt, to taste
limes, extra

1 Separate the octopus tentacles from the head with a sharp knife. Discard the head section and remove the beak from the tentacles. Wash the octopus and dry on absorbent paper.
2 To make marinade: Combine ingredients in a glass, china or other non-metallic bowl, add the octopus tentacles and mix to coat well. Stand for 1 hour, turning occasionally.
3 Preheat barbecue flat plate and spread lightly with oil. Cook the tentacles for 2 minutes, turn and cook further 1 minute or until tender. Serve with buttered bread rolls and extra lime to squeeze over them.
Note: Different brands of liquid smoke can give varying degrees of flavour. If in doubt, use a small amount at first and increase the amount next time you prepare the recipe if you feel it could stand a touch more. Available from some delicatessens.

Tasty Cheese Sticks
Easy to make and will be a great success at any barbecue. You'll need four sheets of ready-rolled puff pastry, 1 cup grated Cheddar cheese, ½ cup finely grated Parmesan cheese and a pinch of chilli powder. Lay two sheets of pastry side by side on a flat work surface, sprinkle each evenly with the cheeses and chilli powder mixed together. Lay the other two sheets of pastry on top and press firmly together with a rolling pin. Cut into strips, about 2 x 12 cm. Twist each strip once and place on a greased baking tray. Brush strips with a little beaten egg and sprinkle with ground sweet paprika. Bake in a hot oven 200°C for 15 minutes or until crisp and golden. Serve warm.

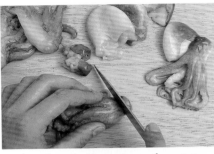

With a sharp knife, separate the octopus tentacles from the head.

Discard the head section and remove the beak from the tentacles.

Combine all the marinade ingredients together in a glass or china bowl.

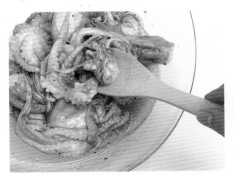

Toss octopus in marinade and mix to coat well. Stand for 1 hour.

Stuffed Mushrooms with Bacon and Cheese

If using an open-style barbecue, place the prepared mushrooms in a shallow metal baking tray and cover with foil. Place the tray on the barbecue flat plate and cook until cheese is golden and melted.

PREPARATION TIME: *20 minutes*
COOKING TIME: *5 minutes*
SERVES 6

3 rashers of bacon, rind removed
½ cup grated mozzarella cheese
1 tablespoon sour cream
½ cup fresh breadcrumbs
1 teaspoon dry English mustard
½ teaspoon ground black pepper

12 large mushroom caps,
stalks removed
1 teaspoon ground sweet paprika

1 Grill the bacon rashers until crisp and chop coarsely. Combine with mozzarella cheese, sour cream, breadcrumbs and English mustard. Season to taste with gound pepper.
2 Spoon the mixture into the mushroom caps. Sprinkle each cap lightly with sweet paprika.
3 Arrange on preheated barbecue grill plate. Cook hood down for 5 minutes or until the cheese melts. Serve immediately.
Note: Do not wash mushrooms before cooking. Simply wipe them clean with a clean, damp cloth. Do not peel them. The mushrooms should be cooked only until tender and cheese melts. If they are over-cooked they will collapse and shrivel before your very eyes. Mushrooms can also be cooked in a moderate oven 180°C for about 8 minutes. Serve the stuffed mushrooms immediately.

Left: Stuffed Mushrooms with Bacon and Cheese. Right: Barbecued Octopus

Serving a selection of cheeses with a variety of crisp crackers is an easy appetiser for lots of people. Choose two or three different cheeses. Some popular choices are Camembert, Pepper Cheese, Cheddar, Smoky Bacon, Edam, Swiss and Jarlsberg cheeses.

Crisp Vegetables with Curry Mayonnaise

Melba Toast
Lay an unsliced stale loaf of white or wholemeal bread on a wooden board and cut in half to give two equal pieces. Remove the crusts from each piece. Turn each portion onto the square end and cut diagonally in half to form two triangular pieces. Thinly slice each piece and lay on a baking tray. Bake in a slow oven 150°C until completely dried and pale golden. Serve with dips.

This recipe is easy to double and will store well in an airtight jar in the refrigerator. It can also be used as a spicy dressing for a simple potato salad.

PREPARATION TIME: *25 minutes*
COOKING TIME: *Nil*
SERVES 6-8

2 sticks celery
12 spring onions
10-12 small red radishes
375 g white button mushrooms
24 sugar or snow peas

CURRY MAYONNAISE
1½ cups mayonnaise
2 teaspoons curry powder
1 teaspoon crushed garlic
2 teaspoons hot chilli sauce
½ teaspoon ground black pepper

1 Cut celery into 8 cm pieces and make fine cuts in one end almost through to the opposite end. Place in cold water and allow to curl. Repeat with the spring onions.
2 Trim and wash radishes. Wipe mushrooms with absorbent paper. Top and tail and string sugar peas or snow peas. Arrange all the prepared vegetables on a large serving platter.
3 To make Curry Mayonnaise: Combine all ingredients thoroughly. Serve in a small bowl with the platter of vegetables.

Crisp Vegetables with Curry Mayonnaise

Blue Cheese and Chive Dip

Serve dips with water crackers, toasted bagels, pitta bread, chips, crudites (sliced raw vegetables) or Melba Toast.

PREPARATION TIME: *10 minutes*
COOKING TIME: *Nil*
SERVES 4-6

125 g cream cheese, softened
¾ cup sour cream
1 tablespoon blue vein cheese
2 tablespoons chopped fresh chives

Blend softened cream cheese and sour cream. Mash blue cheese with a fork and stir it well into cream cheese mixture. Swirl through chopped chives.

Smoked Trout Dip

Smoked trout is available at seafood shops and some delicatessens. Only a small amount is used, but the flavour of this dip is something your guests will not forget.

PREPARATION TIME: *15 minutes*
COOKING TIME: *Nil*
SERVES 4-6

1 x 250 g smoked trout

2 tablespoons sour cream
2 teaspoons lime juice
1 clove garlic, crushed
½ teaspoon ground black pepper
3 tablespoons milk

1 Remove skin and bones from the smoked trout. Flake the flesh of the trout and place in a food processor or blender with remaining ingredients. Blend until smooth. Place in a small bowl, cover with plastic wrap and chill until serving.
2 Serve with crisp crackers or crusty French bread.
Note: If a food processor or blender is not available, flake the trout well and mix with the remaining ingredients, using a fork. The texture will be slightly different.

Above: Smoked Trout Dip. Below: Blue Cheese and Chive Dip

Frankfurt Rolls

Quick and easy savouries that will be a hit with younger guests at a barbecue. Simply spread sheets of ready-rolled puff pastry with mustard, sprinkle lightly with grated cheese. Cut each sheet into two strips and roll thin frankfurts in the pastry to completely enclose. Cut into 5 cm pieces, place on a greased baking tray and brush with a little beaten egg. Bake in a hot oven 200°C for 15-20 minutes or until crisp and golden.

Wildfire Savoury Nuts

Make double quantities of this. As its name implies, this appetiser will disappear like wild-fire.

PREPARATION TIME: *25 minutes*
COOKING TIME: *20 minutes*
SERVES 8

2 tablespoons oil
1 teaspoon garam masala
2 teaspoons garlic powder
½ teaspoon chilli powder
1½ cups salted roasted cashews or peanuts
1½ cups pecan nuts

1 Place oil, garam masala, garlic powder, chilli powder and nuts into a heat resistant baking tray. Stir to coat.
2 Place tray on rack over preheated flat plate. Cook, tossing occasionally, for about 5 minutes. Remove from heat, cool before serving.
Note: Garam masala is available from most Indian and Asian food stores.

Wildfire Savoury Nuts

Vegetable Salad with Simple Satay Sauce

The crunchy textured Satay Sauce gives a new dimension to the vegetables and protein-rich bean curd.

PREPARATION TIME: *30 minutes*
COOKING TIME: *Nil*
SERVES: *10*

6 hard-boiled eggs
4 Lebanese cucumbers
4 large potatoes
250 g pressed bean curd
oil, for frying
2 large carrots, cut into strips
250 g tender green beans
3 cups broccoli florets

SIMPLE SATAY SAUCE
1½ cups crunchy peanut butter
2 tablespoons soy sauce
1 tablespoon sambal olek
2 teaspoons garlic powder
2 teaspoons onion powder
2 tablespoons brown sugar
1 teaspoon shrimp sauce (optional)
½ cup canned coconut milk
extra ½ cup water, for thinning

1 Halve hard-boiled eggs, slice cucumbers lengthways, peel and slice potatoes. Cook potatoes until just tender. Arrange on a large serving platter.
2 Cut bean curd into 3 cm cubes, deep-fry until golden brown and drain on absorbent paper. Allow to cool and place on serving platter.
3 Blanch carrots, green beans and broccoli florets in boiling water until just tender. Drain well and cool before placing on the serving platter.
4 Heat peanut butter in a small pan with the remaining ingredients, using the water to thin if required. Serve in a small bowl with the prepared vegetables.
Note: Shrimp sauce is a pungent condiment that is available at all Asian grocers and gourmet food stores. Anchovy sauce can be used as an alternative. Sambal olek is a fiery chilli condiment made from red chillies and vinegar. If unavailable use a small fresh chilli, finely chopped.

Barbecued Creole Popcorn

Just the thing to enjoy with a few drinks around the barbecue while the chef attends to the main meal. Popping corn is available from supermarkets and health food stores. Store the remaining unpopped corn in an airtight container in a cool, dark, place. Take care to shake the corn as it cooks.

PREPARATION TIME: *15 minutes*
COOKING TIME: *5 minutes*
SERVES: *4-6*

4 tablespoons popping corn
1 tablespoon oil
2 teaspoons Creole Seasoning Mix
(see Note)
30 g butter, melted

1 Using a double layer of heavy-duty or industrial-strength foil, make a basket. Place popcorn and oil in the base.
2 Bring the foil together at the top to make a completely sealed parcel, with enough room for expansion.
3 Place on a preheated barbecue grill. Cook, shaking the basket frequently with tongs as the popcorn begin to pop. Cook for about 5 minutes or until the popcorn ceases to pop. Remove from the grill.
4 Open the parcel, add the melted butter and seasoning mix. Mix well. Serve Creole Popcorn immediately.
Note: To make Creole Seasoning Mix: Combine 1 tablespoon onion powder, 2 tablespoons ground sweet paprika, 1 teaspoon chilli powder, 1 tablespoon ground pepper, 1 tablespoon garlic powder, 2 teaspoons ground dried oregano and 1 tablespoon salt in a small bowl. Store in a covered container in freezer. Use as required. Great to sprinkle on fish and meat dishes. Makes about six tablespoons.

Right: Vegetable Salad with Simple Satay Sauce. Left: Barbecued Creole Popcorn

Tangy Claytons Soda
Pour a generous measure of Claytons non-alcoholic over ice, add an equal amount of lime juice cordial and a slice of lime. Top up with soda water.

THE PERFECT STEAK

There's no excuse for burnt offerings. With a little practice and experimentation you can monitor the 'doneness' of meat with the touch of a finger. Follow our steps to a perfectly cooked steak and you'll never look back!

Rare: Soft to touch, red centre and thin edge of cooked meat.

Choose good quality lean steak, the meat should be of an even thickness to brown and cook evenly. Steaks are best cut to about 3 cm in thickness. If steaks have been marinated and refrigerated allow them to come back to room temperature before barbecuing, this ensures even cooking of meat. Remove excess fat and make small nicks on the edges of each steak to prevent meat curling. Become familiar with the feel of the meat, prod an uncooked steak with your index finger and note its feel. It's soft and offers little resistance to finger pressure.

For a perfectly cooked piece of steak you need first to sear each side to seal in juices. Place the steak on a preheated grill plate, when one surface has been seared (about one minute), sear the other side, use tongs to turn the meat. This firms the surfaces of the meat, retaining the natural juices. If you touch it at this stage it should be about as firm as a semi-dry kitchen sponge and ready to serve to guests who like their steak very rare.

To prepare rare meat, cook only a further minute or two each side. Test the meat with a gentle prod with your index finger, a rare steak should be soft and yielding to touch. The inside of the steak should still be red with a thin edge of cooked meat around it.

For medium-rare, cook a few minutes longer or until slightly springy to the touch. The steak will still be very moist with a slightly thicker edge of cooked meat and a paler red centre.

For a medium steak, cook the steak a further two minutes each side. The steak will be firmer to touch with only a little pinkness in the centre and have a crisp brown outside, they will still be quite juicy inside.

Well-done needs a little more time, the meat will be firm to touch, with a rich brown outside and an evenly cooked centre. At this stage don't make the mistake of cooking it any longer – until all the bounce has gone out of the meat – or it will be as tough and unappetising as army boots.

Medium Rare: Springy to touch, with moist, pale red centre.

STEPS TO A PERFECTLY COOKED STEAK

1 Choose steaks of an even thickness, about 3 cm thick is best.
2 After refrigeration allow meat to come back to room temperature before barbecuing, this ensures even cooking of meat.
3 Sear meat on a preheated barbecue plate for one minute each side. This firms the surfaces of the meat, retaining natural juices. Turn the meat once only.
4 Continue to cook steaks on flat plate, you may need to move the steaks to a cooler part of the barbecue to continue cooking. To test meat for doneness, press the steak with your index finger.
Rare meat will be soft, a medium steak springy and a well-done steak will be firm to touch.
5 Don't feel embarrassed about touching the food in front of your guests – how else do you think restaurant chefs tell when food is done to perfection?
6 When turning steaks or any meats on the barbecue always use tongs, never a fork, as a fork punctures meat and releases juices. This causes flare-ups and it also toughens the meats.

Medium: Firm to touch, pink in centre and crisp, brown edges.

Well-done: Firm, brown outside, evenly cooked centre.

FLAVOURED BUTTERS

Flavoured butters can add a nice finishing touch to a meal and take the place of a sauce. Make a selection of butters and store in the freezer. Allow to soften slightly at room temperature before serving. All butters are prepared in the same way. Soften butter at room temperature and combine with the remaining ingredients. Chill before use in a small butter container or form into a roll and wrap tightly in freezer wrap.

1. For Flavoured Butters: Soften butter. Beat until creamy.

Rosemary Butter

MAKES ½ cup
USES: *Lamb and other meats*

125 g butter, softened
2 tablespoons chopped
fresh rosemary
squeeze lime juice
¼ teaspoon ground pepper

Mustard Butter

MAKES 1⅓ cups
USES: *Beef, poultry and game*

250 g butter, softened
1 tablespoon hot
English mustard
2 tablespoons snipped chives
½ teaspoon crushed garlic

Cheese and Herb Butter

MAKES 1⅓ cups
USES: *Barbecued vegetables*

250 g butter, softened
3 tablespoons grated
Cheddar cheese
3 tablespoons grated
Parmesan cheese
1 tablespoon grated onion
1 tablespoon finely
chopped parsley
1 tablespoon finely chopped basil
½ teaspoon crushed garlic
½ teaspoon ground
black pepper

Garlic Butter

MAKES 1 cup
USES: *Hot bread rolls, potatoes, seafood and steaks*

250 g butter, softened
3 teaspoons crushed garlic
1 tablespoon finely
chopped parsley
¼ teaspoon ground pepper
Tabasco sauce, to taste

Chilli Butter

MAKES 1 cup
USES: *Burgers, steaks and sausages*

125 g butter, softened
1 tablespoon hot chilli sauce
1 teaspoon crushed garlic
1 teaspoon ground sweet paprika
1 teaspoon garam masala
Tabasco sauce, to taste

Herb Butter

MAKES ¾ cup
USES: *Steaks, chicken, fish, vegetables and hot breads or rolls*

125 g butter, softened
1 tablespoon finely chopped
spring onions
2 tablespoons chopped fresh
parsley
1 tablespoon snipped
fresh chives
or 2 teaspoons dried
mixed herbs
¼ teaspoon white pepper

2. Add remaining ingredients. Use any flavourings, mix well.

3. Place in a butter container or shape into a log shape.

4. Refrigerate before use. Slice into 1 cm thick rounds to serve.

Sizzling Beef, Lamb & Pork

Beef is always popular at barbecues and outdoor parties. Tender steaks, juicy roasts and premium ground beef made into skinless sausages and flavoured burgers are all favourites and play an important part in a successful barbecue gathering.

Succulent and tender, lamb is delicious barbecued either pink or well done. But be careful to avoid mutton, the older relative, which could prove tougher, take much longer to cook and is really only suited to long braising or simmering.

Pork is a good choice when barbecuing. It marries well with Asian-style ingredients like soy sauce, ginger and sesame oil to produce tender satays, burgers and finger lickin' ribs. Whatever you decide to choose for your next barbecue, you can't go wrong with any of the beef, lamb and pork recipes that follow.

Left: Beef Satays (page 25). Right: Beef Teriyaki with Onion Rings (page 25)

Korean Beef Ribs

These Korean Beef Ribs can be served as an appetiser or main meal.

PREPARATION TIME: *20 minutes +
4-6 hours marinating*
COOKING TIME: *15 minutes*
SERVES 6

2 kg beef short ribs or pork ribs
½ cup soy sauce
½ cup water
1 onion, grated
3 cloves garlic, crushed
1 teaspoon grated fresh ginger
1 tablespoon sugar
2 teaspoons oriental sesame oil (see Note)
2 tablespoons toasted
sesame seeds, crushed
½ teaspoon ground pepper

1 When purchasing the meat, ask the butcher to cut the ribs into 5 cm squares. Using a sharp knife, cut through the flesh of each piece to allow the marinade to penetrate.
2 Place the ribs in a pan and cover with water, bring to the boil, cover and simmer for 5 minutes. Drain well. This runs off some of the fat.

3 Combine the remaining ingredients in a bowl and add the ribs, mix well, cover and marinate refrigerated for 4-6 hours or overnight. Turn the ribs occasionally while marinating, so that the flavours are evenly distributed.
4 Cook the ribs over a hot oiled grill, allow each side to brown and become crisp. Serve warm.
Note: Most supermarkets have oriental sesame oil (which is made from dark roasted sesame seeds) on their Asian shelves. Or look for it at your local Asian food outlet. Light sesame oil from the health food store will not do.

The best beef cuts for barbecue roasting are whole pieces of rib eye, a thick slice of rump and boneless sirloin. If you're marinating meats for the barbecue, economical cuts which give good results include the first 4-5 slices of round, topside and silverside. Rib steak, bone-in-blade, oyster blade and beef spare ribs are also good choices.

Korean Beef Ribs

Using a sharp knife, cut through the flesh of each rib piece.

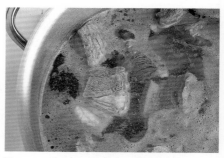

Simmer ribs in pan of water for 5 minutes and drain well.

Place ribs in a bowl with remaining ingredients, mix well and cover.

Beef Satays

Barbecued food on a stick is something very special and is responsible for the immense popularity of the Satay Club of Singapore where the delicious peanut sauce surrounding char-grilled meat is a taste to experience. This superb satay recipe will allow you to experience the Singapore Satay flavour right in your own backyard.

PREPARATION TIME: *15 minutes +*
1 hour marinating
COOKING TIME: *10 minutes*
SERVES 6

750 g rump steak

MARINADE
½ teaspoon grated lemon rind
1 onion, grated
2 tablespoons soy sauce
1 tablespoons peanut oil
2 teaspoons ground coriander
1 teaspoon ground cumin
1 teaspoon ground turmeric
1 clove garlic, crushed
1 teaspoon brown sugar
2 tablespoons crunchy peanut butter

SIMPLE SATAY SAUCE
1½ cups crunchy peanut butter
2 tablespoons soy sauce
1 tablespoon sambal olek or chilli sauce
2 teaspoons garlic powder
2 teaspoons onion powder
2 tablespoons brown sugar
1 teaspoon shrimp sauce (optional)
½ cup canned coconut milk
extra ½ cup water, for thinning

1 Cut the rump steak into small cubes, about 1 cm square.
2 To make Marinade: Place all the ingredients in a small bowl and mix well or blend in a food processor or blender until smooth. Pour over the prepared meat and allow to marinate for 1 hour.
3 Thread meat onto soaked bamboo skewers, allowing a little room between each one and leaving about half the skewer free. Cover and refrigerate until ready to barbecue.
4 To make Simple Satay Sauce: Heat peanut butter in a small pan together with the remaining ingredients, using the water

to thin it down to a pouring consistency. Use as desired. Serve warm.
5 When ready to serve, cook satays over a moderate preheated barbecue, turning occasionally until nicely browned. Serve with satay sauce.
Note: To make Satay Kambing (lamb satays): Use well trimmed lamb, as a substitute for beef in this recipe. Satays are always served well cooked, never rare.

Beef Teriyaki with Onion Rings

Select the finest cut of Scotch fillet with a light marbling of fat through it. You can then be sure of a tender and tasty result.

PREPARATION TIME: *20 minutes +*
15 minutes marinating
COOKING TIME: *15 minutes*
SERVES 8

**8 x 1.5 cm slices Scotch fillet
or fillet steak**
½ cup mirin or dry sherry
½ cup soy sauce
1 clove garlic, crushed
1 teaspoon grated fresh ginger
½ teaspoon ground pepper

ONION RINGS
4 large white onions
2 tablespoons sunflower oil
2 tablespoons beef marinade

1 Marinate beef slices in the combined mirin, soy, garlic, ginger and pepper for 15 minutes. Preheat the barbecue.
2 Peel onions and cut into 1.5 cm thick slices. Drizzle oil on flat plate. Cook onion rings until golden, sprinkle with marinade and continue to cook until caramelised – about 5 minutes. Remove to a cooler part of the flat plate and keep warm.
3 Oil the flat plate and cook the beef on high heat for 5 minutes on one side and 3 minutes on the reverse, cooking for an increased time if a well done steak is preferred. Serve meat with barbecued onion rings.
Note: Mirin is available from good delicatessens and Japanese food outlets. Dry sherry can be used in its place.

Satays are a great way to start your barbecue meal. Make them small on short soaked bamboo skewers. If available, cook them on a small table-top or hibachi barbecue. Guests can cook their own and it leaves valuable space on the barbecue for the main meal. Serve with lots of peanut sauce.

Roast Beef with Pecan Sauce

Allow large cuts of meat to rest for 15 minutes before carving. This allows the flesh to relax and saves juices from running out.

When you feel like a roast and the weather is warm, why heat up your kitchen? With a kettle or hooded barbecue you can prepare a wonderful roast. Serve with jacket potatoes hot from the coals, and barbecued corn cobs. The time allowed should result in a rare roast. If you prefer the meat medium or well done, simply allow extra cooking time.

PREPARATION TIME: *25 minutes +*
30 minutes standing
COOKING TIME: *1½ hours*
SERVES *8*

ROAST
1 x 2.5 kg rib of roasting beef
1 medium onion, grated
1 clove garlic, crushed
½ teaspoon ground pepper
1 teaspoon ground dried oregano

SAUCE
½ cup pecans, toasted (see Note)
1 cup water
2 teaspoons beef stock powder
¼ teaspoon ground pepper
30 g unsalted butter
2 tablespoons plain flour

1 cup soaked hickory
wood chips (optional)

1 Slash rib meat, mix all ingredients together and spread over roast. Let stand for 30 minutes while making sauce.
2 To make Sauce: Place toasted pecans in a blender jar together with water, stock powder and pepper. Blend to a paste.
3 Melt butter in a small pan, add the flour and mix to a paste. Cook, stirring occasionally for 5-6 minutes or until golden. Remove from the heat and add the pecan mixture blend gradually. Return to the heat and stir until the mixture simmers and thickens.
4 Cooking the roast: Heat the barbecue kettle, place rib on a rack in a dish, with 1½ cups water. Place on the grill plate, cover and cook for about 2 hours, basting every 30 minutes with the sauce. If using, hickory chips add the chips to barbecue during the final ½ hour of cooking time.
5 When done to your preference, remove roast to a serving dish and serve with remaining sauce and roast potatoes.
Note: To toast pecans: Place on a baking tray and heat in a moderate oven 180°C for 10 minutes or until crisp. Shake the tray occasionally to avoid burning.

Beef Balls in Barbecue Sauce

These tasty beef morsels are great with fresh bread rolls and salad. If preferred, place two or three onto short bamboo skewers and cook, turning the skewers occasionally. For a quick appetiser, place on toothpicks and serve with extra barbecue sauce as a dip.

PREPARATION TIME: *15 minutes*
COOKING TIME: *6 minutes*
SERVES *6*

500 g premium mince beef
1 egg
1 medium onion,
finely chopped
1 clove garlic, crushed
1 teaspoon grated fresh ginger
salt and pepper, to taste
1 cup bottled barbecue sauce
(see Note)

1 Place mince, egg, onion, garlic, ginger, salt and pepper. Combine throughly by hand. Take level tablespoonsful of mince mixture and roll into balls.
2 Place on well oiled, hot barbecue flat plate and cook for 5-6 minutes, moving them around occasionally.
3 Brush meatballs liberally with barbecue basting sauce 1 minute before the end of cooking. Serve immediately with remaining barbecue sauce.
Note: Bottled barbecue sauce is available in most supermarkets. It has a mild hickory smoked flavour. If not available, use your favourite homemade barbecue sauce.

Left: Roast Beef with Pecan Sauce. Right: Beef Balls in Barbecue Sauce

Smoky Beef Sausages

When little preparation time is available, buy a selection of flavoured sausages from a specialty shop. Blanch sausages first and prick lightly with a slender skewer to prevent skins bursting. Barbecue and serve with salads.

These skinless sausages are great served in warm rolls with salad.

PREPARATION TIME: *20 minutes +*
overnight refrigeration
COOKING TIME: *15 minutes*
SERVES 6-8

1 kg premium mince beef
1 egg
¾ cup water
1 teaspoon salt
2 teaspoons cracked black peppercorns
2 teaspoons toasted coriander seeds
3 cloves garlic, crushed
2 tablespoons bottled barbecue sauce
1 onion, grated
1 tablespoon hot chilli sauce or few shakes Tabasco sauce

1 Combine all the ingredients in a large bowl, beating with a wooden spoon until all the water is absorbed. If necessary, mix with hands to distribute all the spices and seasonings evenly.
2 Divide the mixture into eight equal portions. Place each portion on a large sheet of greaseproof paper and roll into a cylinder shape. Refrigerate overnight.
3 Remove sausages from the paper, cook on a lightly oiled preheated grill, turning once during cooking. Serve immediately with a crisp green salad.

Smoky Beef Sausages

Thai Beef Salad

The herbs in this salad give it a lovely fresh flavour. Fresh kaffir lime leaves, if you can get them, make it really special.

PREPARATION TIME: *10 minutes*
COOKING TIME: *3-5 minutes*
SERVES 4-6

500 g rump or fillet steak

DRESSING
1 clove garlic, crushed
2 teaspoons palm sugar or brown sugar
1 tablespoon fish sauce
1 tablespoon white vinegar
2 teaspoons grated lemon or lime rind
2 tablespoons lime juice

SALAD
2 spring onions, sliced
1 small red capsicum, diced
2 small seedless cucumbers, thickly sliced
½ cup finely chopped coriander leaves and stems
½ cup shredded mint
½ cup shredded basil
1 tender stem of lemongrass, thinly sliced
or 2 teaspoons grated lemon rind
1 red chilli, finely shredded
3 fresh kaffir lime leaves, cut into threads (optional)

1 Trim any excess fat from the steak.
2 To make Dressing: Combine all the ingredients in a screwtop jar and shake well.
3 To make Salad: Combine all the prepared salad ingredients in a large bowl, cover tightly with plastic wrap and chill until serving time.
4 To cook meat: Sear over high heat on a lightly oiled barbecue flat plate. Cook to your taste. Best results with this salad are with moist, juicy rare to medium rare steak. Remove from the barbecue, allow to rest for 10 minutes and slice thinly. Combine meat slices with salad and dressing, toss well to distribute the flavours. Serve immediately.
Note: If Kaffir lime leaves are not available, use very tender citrus leaves – either lemon or Tahitian lime – instead, though the fragrance is not quite the same.

Above: Thai Beef Salad. Below: Moroccan Koftas (page 30)

29

Hamburgers are most popular, especially with the young ones. Shape round and 2 cm thick. Place eight or more in a hamburger frame and cook on hot coals for 3 minutes each side, turning once for a medium result. Versions and flavours are as numerous as your imagination. You may like to include garlic powder, chopped spring onions or coriander, Worcestershire sauce, sweet chilli sauce or a spicy hickory flavoured barbecue sauce.

Hamburgers Supreme

Hamburgers Supreme

These extra tasty hamburgers, will be a real hit with the teenagers. Serve with bread rolls, thick slices of tomato, onion rings, shredded lettuce and, of course, tomato sauce. Let everyone assemble their own to their own specifications.

PREPARATION TIME: *20 minutes +
30 minutes standing*
COOKING TIME: *30 minutes*
SERVES 4

¼ cup medium cracked wheat (burghul)
1 medium onion, finely chopped
½ teaspoon ground dried oregano leaves
1 clove garlic, crushed
salt and pepper, to taste
2 tablespoons Worcestershire sauce
1 teaspoon ground coriander
500 g beef mince
1 egg

1 Soak burghul in hot water for 30 minutes. Drain and squeeze out excess water. Place into a large mixing bowl. Add onion, oregano, garlic, salt and pepper, Worcestershire sauce, coriander, mince and egg. Mix thoroughly to combine.

2 Form mixture into ⅓ cup amounts, flatten slightly and place on a tray.
3 Heat barbecue and when hot, oil the flat plate and cook patties about 8-10 minutes each side or until done. Serve with salad and bread rolls.
Note: Burghul, also known as cracked wheat, is a great way to add fibre to a meal, it will also help to extend the main ingredient.

Moroccan Koftas

This recipe may be cooked on an open-style barbecue or a kettle barbecue. Allow slightly longer cooking time if using an open-style barbecue.

PREPARATION TIME: *15 minutes*
COOKING TIME: *8 minutes*
SERVES 6

750 g premium minced beef
1 egg
½ cup finely chopped fresh coriander or parsley
salt and pepper, to taste
2 teaspoons ground coriander
2 teaspoons ground cumin
1 teaspoon chilli powder
2 teaspoons ground sweet paprika
½ teaspoon ground turmeric
1 medium onion, grated
½ teaspoon ground cinnamon

water-soaked grape or
cherry wood (optional)

1 Combine all ingredients together and form into sausage shapes around skewers, or make into hamburger shapes.
2 Heat kettle barbecue on medium high. Place soaked grape or cherry wood over grill, if using, and oil flat plate.
3 Place skewered koftas on flat plate and cook 4 minutes each side covered, making sure the fruit wood burns and gives off its particular aroma. Serve with Lavash or Middle Eastern bread, sliced tomatoes and raw onion rings.
Note: Turmeric, a member of the onion family, is an orange-yellow coloured spice used to add colour and flavour. Like all spices and herbs, store in an airtight container away from direct sunlight.

Spicy Rotisserie Leg of Lamb

When cooking a large joint of meat, it is best to use a covered barbecue. If one of these is not available, make a wind shield of heavy-duty foil, otherwise be prepared for the cooking to take quite a bit longer.

PREPARATON TIME: *10 minutes +*
1 hour marinating
COOKING TIME: *1½ hours*
SERVES 8

1 x 2 kg leg of lamb

MARINADE
2 teaspoons ground turmeric
1 teaspoon ground sweet paprika
salt and pepper, to taste
2 large cloves garlic, crushed
1 teaspoon grated fresh ginger
3 tablespoons yoghurt
1 teaspoon ground cardamom

1 Trim off excess fat and score the leg of lamb with shallow diagonal cuts 3 cm apart on both sides.
2 To make Marinade: Combine all the ingredients and spread over the lamb, making sure to fill the criss-cross cuts. Marinate for 1 hour or overnight in the refrigerator.
3 Heat covered gas barbecue. Skewer lamb and attach to rotisserie, taking care to balance the leg of lamb so weight is evenly distributed or rotisserie will not turn smoothly. Cook 1½ hours over low heat until done to your liking. Baste with remaining marinade every 15 minutes.

Barbecue Rack of Lamb

This quick, easy barbecue rack of lamb recipe is a boon when you are short of time as it uses dried herbs and spices. Best cooked on a kettle barbecue.

PREPARATON TIME: *10 minutes +*
30 minutes marinating
COOKING TIME: *25 minutes*
SERVES 8

Spicy Rotisserie Leg of Lamb

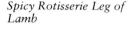

8 racks of lamb,
each with 3-4 ribs

DRY MARINADE
2 teaspoons onion powder
1 teaspoon garlic powder
2 teaspoons dried mint leaves
1 teaspoon lemon pepper seasoning
salt, to taste

1 Trim the racks of excess fat. Separate the bones at the end of each rack, scrape away any flesh or fat to leave about 4 cm of cleaned bone at the end of each cutlet.
2 To make Dry Marinade: Combine all ingredients and rub over the meat. Allow to marinate for about 30 minutes.
3 Preheat the kettle barbecue and cook lamb racks over lightly oiled surface for 20-25 minutes or until done to your liking. Serve racks of lamb with potatoes and mint jelly or sauce.
Note: Onion powder, mint flakes, garlic powder and lemon seasoning are all available from supermarket spice racks. Experiment with different combinations of herbs.

Avoid using forks to turn meat on the barbecue. Use tongs or implements which won't pierce the meat and cause loss of juices during cooking

Roasts are preferably rotisseried or cooked over indirect heat. Use medium heat to ensure the roasts are evenly cooked and excess juices are not lost, by excessive shrinkage. Check the temperature of the roast with a meat thermometer to assess the progress of cooking. Later during the cooking process you can check the 'doneness' using a fine metal skewer.

Lamb Chops Indienne

Lamb Chops Indienne

A spicy marinade with the accent on speed and ease of preparation adds interest to an everyday ingredient. Serve the lamb chops with mango chutney.

PREPARATION TIME: *10 minutes +*
1 hour marinating
COOKING TIME: *6-8 minutes*
SERVES 6

12 lamb chops, excess fat removed

MARINADE
2 teaspoons curry powder
1 teaspoon garam masala
1 teaspoon garlic powder
2 teaspoons onion powder
1 tablespoon white vinegar
salt, to taste
3 tablespoons water
2 tablespoons oil

1 To make Marinade: Combine all ingredients and spread evenly over lamb chops. Allow the meat to marinate 1 hour or overnight in refrigerator.
2 Heat barbecue to medium and place marinated lamb chops on oiled flat or grill plate. Cook for 5 minutes, turn and cook for a further 3 minutes. Cook further according to taste if required.
Note: Garam masala can be purchased in supermarkets and Indian food stores.

Smoked Leg of Lamb

For this recipe the lamb is rotisseried in a kettle or covered barbecue. If cooked by any other method it will not have quite the same wonderful results.

PREPARATION TIME: *10 minutes +*
1 hour marinating
COOKING TIME: *1½ hours*
SERVES 6-8

1.5 kg leg of lamb,
excess fat removed
3 cups mesquite or
hickory chips, soaked (optional)

MARINADE
2 teaspoons ground sweet paprika
½ teaspoon ground pepper
salt, to taste
1 teaspoon ground dried mint flakes
3 cloves garlic, crushed
1 teaspoon ground cumin
1 tablespoon ground rice
2 - 3 tablespoons water

1 Put the mesquite or hickory chips, if using, to soak in cold water before starting preparation of the food.
2 To make Marinade: Combine all ingredients. Score the lamb with shallow diagonal slashes to form diamond shapes and spread marinade making sure it gets into all the slashes. Cover and let stand 1 hour or overnight in the refrigerator.
3 Heat barbecue, skewer lamb securely and attach to rotisserie.
4 Bake with the hood down on low heat for about 1½ hours, basting with the leftover marinade. Add two handfuls of soaked chips to glowing coals every 30 minutes, if using.
5 When the meat is done to your liking remove the rotisserie spit from the barbecue and let the meat stand for 10 minutes before serving. Serve the smoked leg of lamb with vegetables of your choice, or spiced rice.
Note: Marinated meats should be at room temperature before barbecuing to allow for even cooking, and for the meat to absorb extra flavour. If not, the outside may be overcooked while the inside is still raw.

Above: Smoked Leg of Lamb. Below: Lamb Kebabs (page 34)

If you've been elected to hold the annual get together with stacks of people, prepare all the food for the barbecue and cover with plastic wrap. Place small trays of food near the barbecue and allow guests to cook their own. This not only allows them to cook their meal the way they like, but they can also eat at their leisure. Meanwhile you're free to attend to drinks, top up the food supply and enjoy the party.

Butterflied Leg of Lamb

Butterflied Leg of Lamb

Ask the butcher to bone and butterfly the leg of lamb to make the preparation of this dish much easier.

PREPARATION TIME: *20 minutes +
30 minutes marinating*
COOKING TIME: *25 minutes*
SERVES 6-8

**1 x 1.5 kg leg of lamb, boned and
butterflied**

**MARINADE
2 teaspoons ground dried mint
2 cloves garlic, crushed
1 tablespoon olive oil
1 tablespoon pickled green peppercorns,
mashed (see Note)
salt and pepper, to taste**

1 Trim off excess fat and lay the boned leg of lamb on a flat surface. Score the inside, criss-cross fashion. Turn the lamb and repeat with the other side.
2 To make Marinade: Combine all ingredients and rub into the scored surfaces. Allow the meat to marinate, covered, for at least 30 minutes or overnight.

3 Place lamb on a lightly oiled preheated barbecue grill and cook for 20-25 minutes, turning once during cooking for a rare result. Increase the cooking time if you prefer lamb well done. Allow meat to stand for 15 minutes before slicing.
Note: Pickled green peppercorns are available at delicatessens and some supermarkets. Store remaining peppercorns and brine in an airtight jar, refrigerated.
To reduce flareups place a foil tray directly under the lamb to catch melted fat.

Lamb Kebabs

Halve preparation time by asking the butcher to bone the leg for you.

PREPARATION TIME: *30 minutes +
overnight marinating*
COOKING TIME: *10 minutes*
SERVES 6

1 x 1.5 kg leg of lamb, boned

**MARINADE
2 teaspoons grated fresh ginger
(see Note)
2 cloves garlic, crushed
salt and pepper, to taste
3 teaspoons ground coriander
2 teaspoons ground cumin
2 teaspoons ground turmeric
½ teaspoon ground nutmeg
½ teaspoon ground cardamom
1 teaspoon white vinegar
2 tablespoons peanut oil**

1 Trim any excess fat from the lamb and cut into 2.5 cm cubes.
2 To make Marinade: Combine all ingredients in a medium-sized bowl.
3 Add lamb, and stir to coat with spice mix. Cover and refrigerate overnight.
4 Thread each skewer with four to five pieces of lamb, and barbecue on a lightly oiled preheated barbecue grill or flat plate. Cook until well-browned, turning gradually. Serve with pitta bread or rice and a sauce of finely chopped cucumber and yoghurt.
Note: Fresh grated ginger adds a distinct flavour to this recipe. If unavailable in your area, good quality, ready minced ginger can be purchased in supermarkets.

Lamb Fillets with Ginger

Serve these with hot steamed rice or even pop the Lamb Fillets with Ginger into crusty bread rolls.

PREPARATION TIME: *20 minutes +*
30 minutes marinating
COOKING TIME: *10 minutes*
SERVES 6

12 small lamb loin fillets

MARINADE
2 cloves garlic, crushed
2 teaspoons grated fresh ginger
2 spring onions, finely chopped
1 tablespoon Korean chilli paste
**2 tablespoons toasted sesame
seeds, crushed**
1 teaspoon ground pepper
1 tablespoon water
2 teaspoons oriental sesame oil

1 Use a sharp knife to remove the silvery sinew from the outside of each lamb fillet. Split the fillets almost in half lengthways, leaving them joined, and open them out so they are flat.
2 To make Marinade: Combine all ingredients thoroughly. Pour over the fillets, mix and leave to marinate for 30 minutes or longer in the refrigerator.
3 Cook on a preheated barbecue grill, over medium high heat for 3 minutes on each side or until done. Serve with your favourite salad.
Note: Adjust the quantity of chilli paste to suit your taste.

Spicy Lamb Sausages

A spicy, skinless sausage for the barbecue. For those that really like it hot, serve with extra chilli sauce.

PREPARATION TIME: *40 minutes +*
30 minutes soaking
COOKING TIME: *6 minutes*
SERVES 8

Spicy Lamb Sausages

**½ cup medium or coarse cracked
wheat (burghul)**
500 g minced lamb
1 egg
1 medium onion, grated
2 cloves garlic, crushed
1 teaspoon ground cumin
2 tablespoons harissa (see Note)
½ teaspoon ground pepper
¼ cup chopped fresh coriander

1 Soak burghul in water for 30 minutes, drain and squeeze out excess water.
2 Using your hands, combine burghul with remaining ingredients.
3 Divide the meat mixture into eight and form each into a long sausage shape around flat metal skewers.
4 Cook on a preheated flat plate for about 3 minutes each side or until done.
Note: Harissa is a hot, chilli-based sauce. To make your own Harissa: Combine 4 tablespoons hot chilli sauce in a small bowl with 1 tablespoon garlic powder, 2 teaspoons ground coriander, 2 teaspoons ground cumin and 2 teaspoons ground dried mint, 1 teaspoon salt and 2 tablespoons finely chopped fresh coriander. Makes about ½ cup.

Always heat the flat plate or grill first and then brush lightly with oil before cooking your barbecue food. This will prevent your meats from catching. Make sure that the brush you use won't melt in the heat ... in other words, not one made of nylon bristles or your flat plate cooked foods will have an unwanted, unpleasant flavour.

To reduce the cooking time of sausages on the barbecue, place sausages in a large pan, cover with water and bring slowly to simmering point. Simmer for 1-2 minutes. Remove from the heat, cool and drain. Store in airtight container. Barbecue briefly to brown and complete the cooking. Barbecued sausages served in hot buttered rolls, topped with homemade barbecue sauce are always popular with the young ones.

Lamb Burgers

Lamb Burgers

Middle Eastern in flavour, these tasty meat patties are always popular at barbecue gatherings and easy to prepare.

PREPARATION TIME: *15 minutes +*
20 minutes standing
COOKING TIME: *10 minutes*
SERVES *8*

½ cup fine cracked wheat (burghul)
500 g minced lamb
1 egg
1 large onion, grated
2 teaspoons herb pepper seasoning
½ teaspoon ground cinnamon
½ teaspoon ground dried mint, crumbled

1 Soak the burghul in cold water for 20 minutes or until soft. Drain well and squeeze out all excess moisture.
2 Combine all the ingredients in a bowl and mix thoroughly with the hand to distribute flavours.
3 Form into eight oval patties. Cook in a multi hamburger frame or preheated oiled flat plate for 5 minutes each side or until cooked according to taste.
Note: Hamburger frames, are readily available at barbecue accessory shops, make turning your burgers so easy. They also ensure uniform cooking.

Herbed Lamb

This is best cooked on a kettle barbecue using charcoal or heat beads. If cooking this recipe on an open-style barbecue, you will need to allow extra time for cooking. This marinade can be used on cubes of boned lamb to be skewered or simply use to marinate well-trimmed rib loin lamb cutlets.

PREPARATION TIME: *15 minutes +*
30 minutes marinating
COOKING TIME: *8 minutes*
SERVES *4 - 6*

12 (1 kg) rib loin cutlets

MARINADE
1 clove garlic, crushed
salt and pepper, to taste
1 medium onion, grated
2 tablespoons finely chopped
fresh oregano
2 tablespoons lemon juice
4 tablespoons olive oil

1 cup hickory or cherry
wood chips, soaked (optional)

1 Snip the edges of the cutlets to prevent them from curling. To make Marinade: Combine all the ingredients in a large shallow dish.
2 Turn fillets over in the marinade. Allow to marinate for 30 minutes, turning once.
3 Place chops on preheated barbecue grill plate, add water-soaked wood chips to glowing coals, if using, and cook over medium heat, hood down for 4 minutes. Turn and continue to cook for 3 minutes to give a medium rare result and continue to cook if well done is preferred. Serve with a crisp green salad or barbecued vegetables.
Note: If using wood chips make sure that they are well alight before starting to barbecue the lamb. Trim any excess fat from steaks and chops for the barbecue. Snip the edges of the remaining fat with scissors or a small, sharp knife to prevent the meat from curling.

Left: Herbed Lamb. Right: Lamb Fillets with Ginger (page 35)

Oriental Lamb Fillets

When friends drop in at the last minute, coat steaks with seasoned pepper or crushed peppercorns and barbecue on a lighly oiled flat plate for a quick and easy treat.

Oriental Lamb Fillets

Any type of kebab is ideal for barbecue entertaining. Serve with sliced raw onions and flat bread for a meal in one.

PREPARATION TIME: *20 minutes +*
30 minutes marinating
COOKING TIME: *10 minutes*
SERVES 6

12 small lamb fillets

MARINADE
1 clove garlic, crushed
1 teaspoon grated fresh ginger
1 small onion, peeled and
roughly chopped
1 tablespoon fresh curry leaves (see Note)
¼ teaspoon turmeric
salt and pepper, to taste
1 tablespoon lemon juice
1 tablespoon water
1 teaspoon oriental sesame oil

1 Trim the lamb fillets and remove all the silvery sinews using a sharp knife. Split each of the fillets in half lengthways starting at the tip and leaving the fillet joined at the thick end.

2 To make Marinade: Combine all the ingredients in a blender until smooth. If a blender is not available, grate the onion and finely chop the curry leaves. Combine all ingredients in a small bowl. Pour the marinade over the fillets, mix and leave to marinate for 30 minutes.
3 Thread onto metal skewers ribbon fashion. Cook lamb on preheated grill of the barbecue over medium high heat for 5 minutes each side or until done. Serve with your favourite salad.
Note: Fresh curry leaves can be found in Asian food stores. If not available, substitute fresh oregano or marjoram leaves. The taste is just as delicioius.

Trim the lamb fillets, remove sinews and split in half lengthwise.

Place marinade ingredients in blender and blend until smooth.

Thread marinated lamb strips onto skewers in a ribbon fashion.

Spicy Grilled Lamb

Fillets, or tender loins as they are sometimes called, are delicate flavoured, fat-free portions of lamb that could also be used in this recipe.

PREPARATION TIME: *20 minutes +*
30 minutes marinating
COOKING TIME: *10 minutes*
SERVES 6

6 lamb leg steaks

MARINADE
1 clove garlic, crushed
1 teaspoon grated fresh ginger (see Note)
1 tablespoon lemon juice
1 tablespoon water
½ cup chopped coriander leaves
1 small onion, roughly chopped
¼ teaspoon ground pepper
1 teaspoon mild curry powder
½ teaspoon garam marsala
salt and pepper, to taste

1 Place lamb steaks in a shallow dish.
2 To make Marinade: Combine all the ingredients in a blender or food processor until smooth and pour over the lamb. Allow to marinate for 30 minutes. (If a food processor or blender is unavailable, finely chop the coriander, grate the onion and combine marinade ingredients in a small bowl.)
3 Cook over medium high heat on barbecue grill plate for 5 minutes each side or until rosy pink inside, brown outside. Cut into thick diagonal slices to serve.
Note: If you don't often use fresh ginger, peel and slice a small root, place in a clean jar and cover with dry sherry or green ginger wine. It will keep in the refrigerator for months. The sherry or wine can also be used in Asian-style dishes.

Tandoori-style Lamb

A tandoor is an earthen oven using charcoal as a fire source. This Mongol-initiated style of cooking is adaptable for poultry, meats, fish and even vegetable dishes. Best cooked on a kettle barbecue.

PREPARATION TIME: *10 minutes +*
1 hour marinating
COOKING TIME: *12 minutes*
SERVES 4

12 (1 kg) rib loin cutlets
1 clove garlic, crushed
1 teaspoon grated fresh ginger
½ teaspoon ground pepper
1 teaspoon ground turmeric
1 teaspoon ground sweet paprika
1 teaspoon garam masala
¼ cup plain yoghurt

1 Trim the loin cutlets of any excess fat. Then score the edges of the meat to prevent the cutlets from curling when they are barbecued.
2 Make a paste with all the other ingredients and coat cutlets with marinade. Set aside 1 hour.
3 Preheat the barbecue and cook on the oiled grill plate for 6 minutes on each side.

Above: Spicy Grilled Lamb. Below: Tandoori-style Lamb

Overcrowding the grill can cause an excess of smoke. Leave plenty of room between foods so they can be easily turned and smoke kept to a minimum.

Pork Satays

Ham steaks are a quick and easy barbecue meal. Barbecue steaks and rings of pineapple until golden, brushing steaks with a little combined mustard and pineapple juice toward the end of cooking.

This is a popular snack in Singapore, Thailand and other South East Asian countries. Wonderful for parties. I've found that a good way to break the ice is to let everyone cook their own!

PREPARATION TIME: *20 minutes +*
overnight marinating
COOKING TIME: *10-15 minutes*
SERVES *8-10*

1 kg shoulder pork or pork neck
2 red chillies
1 large onion
2 teaspoons grated fresh ginger
2 teaspoons brown sugar
2 teaspoons turmeric
2 teaspoons ground coriander
1 teaspoon ground cinnamon
2 teaspoons grated lemon rind
2 tablespoons lemon juice
1 tablespoon soy sauce
1 tablespoon peanut oil

Pork Satays

1 Trim pork of skin and fat. Cut meat into small cubes or thin strips. Combine remaining ingredients in a blender and blend to a paste. Alternatively, finely chop chilli, grate the onion and mix with remaining ingredients in a small bowl.
2 Place the meat in a bowl and pour on marinade, stirring to thoroughly coat meat. Cover and refrigerate overnight, to allow flavours to develop. Thread onto soaked bamboo skewers.
3 Grill over a medium-hot barbecue until cooked through. Serve with rice and dipping sauce. Or if more convenient, spread the sauce on crusty rolls split through the middle. Slip the meat off the skewer down the centre of the roll.
Note: To make Dipping Sauce: Combine ½ cup crunchy peanut butter with 1 clove garlic, crushed, 2 teaspoons soy sauce. 2 teaspoons hot chilli sauce, ½ teaspoon oriental sesame oil and ⅓ cup coconut milk.

Pork and Veal Pitta Burgers

A taste-tingling recipe for an adult gathering. Omit the chilli sauce if you are cooking for children.

PREPARATION TIME: *10 minutes*
COOKING TIME: *8 minutes*
SERVES *4-6*

500 g pork and veal mince
1 large onion, grated
salt and pepper, to taste
1 teaspoon ground oregano leaves
1 clove garlic, crushed
1 teaspoon hot chilli sauce
⅓ cup fresh breadcrumbs

1 Combine all ingredients, mix well and divide into six. Shape the mixture into flat, round patties and place on oiled hamburger frame.
2 Barbecue on medium high heat on grill plate for 4 minutes, turn over and cook further 4 minutes. Serve burgers on pitta bread with a mixed salad, sour cream and pickled sour cucumbers.
Note: Ensure you make all of the burgers the same size to allow for even cooking.

Skewered Ginger Pork

Ginger and pork are a great combination and this recipe brings the two together in a delightful dish.

PREPARATION TIME: *20 minutes +*
1 hour marinating
COOKING TIME: *10 minutes*
SERVES 6

500 g pork fillets
2 tablespoons grated fresh ginger
½ teaspoon ground pepper
1 teaspoon oriental sesame oil
1 tablespoon lemon juice
1 small onion, grated
salt and pepper, to taste

1 Cube the pork, combine remaining ingredients and marinate pork for 1 hour.
2 Skewer pork and barbecue on flat plate for 5 minutes each side or until cooked to personal taste. Serve with a salad and hot bread rolls.
Note: Pork fillets are a delicate cut with little fat visible. If not easy to come by, choose another lean cut as a substitute.

Skewered Ginger Pork

Remember to soak bamboo skewers in water for a few hours beforehand or they will cook before your meat does!

Pork and Veal Meatloaf

Cooking veal on the barbecue requires a lot of care. This lean meat can easily dry out, so basting is essential throughout the cooking time.

Cooking a meatloaf on the barbecue! Who would ever imagine it? It's great to cook on the side of the grill while you're cooking up other barbecue fare. Serve meatloaf sliced with a crisp garden salad.

PREPARATION TIME: *10 minutes*
COOKING TIME: *1 hour*
SERVES 6-8

1 kg pork and veal mince
¾ cup bottled plum sauce
1 medium onion, grated
½ cup chopped coriander leaves
2 cloves garlic, crushed
salt and pepper, to taste
2 eggs, lightly beaten
1 cup fresh breadcrumbs

BASTING MIXTURE
2 teaspoons chicken stock powder
2 tablespoons hot water

1 Combine pork and veal mince in a bowl with the remaining meatloaf ingredients.
2 Place the pork and veal mixture in a 21 x 14 x 7 cm lightly greased or non-stick loaf tin.
3 Preheat barbecue and place loaf tin on a rack over the flat plate. Cook with the hood down for 1 hour, basting meatloaf every 15 minutes with combined chicken stock powder and hot water.
4 Serve sliced with a crisp green salad.
Note: Bottled plum sauce can be purchased from supermarkets and Asian stores. Use barbecue sauce as a substitute.

Stars and Stripes Barbecue Ribs

Get the leanest pork spare ribs you can find. Not all butchers prepare them in the American style and fatty ones are prone to cause flareups and burn. The sauce quantity is enough for two batches. Store half in a clean glass jar in the refrigerator.

PREPARATION TIME: *30 minutes + overnight marinating*
COOKING TIME: *15 minutes*
SERVES 6-8

1.5 kg American-style pork spare ribs

SAUCE
1 teaspoon dry mustard, or prepared English mustard
1 teaspoon ground sweet paprika
2 cloves garlic, crushed
1 teaspoon Tabasco sauce
½ teaspoon ground oregano
½ teaspoon ground cumin
3 tablespoons peanut oil
1 cup tomato sauce
⅓ cup tomato paste
⅓ cup brown sugar
2 tablespoons Worcestershire sauce
1 tablespoon brown vinegar

1 To make Sauce: Mix mustard and dry spices with oil in a medium pan. Blend in sauce and remaining ingredients. Cook, stirring, over medium heat for 5 minutes until combined. Cool before refrigerating. Store half for later use.
2 Coat ribs with remaining sauce and marinate overnight. Cook on medium hot barbecue grill, turning frequently, until firm and well done.
Note: This marinade and the sauce are equally good with beef spare ribs. However, if using beef ribs they should be simmered until tender and drained before marinating and barbecuing.

Pork and Veal Meatloaf

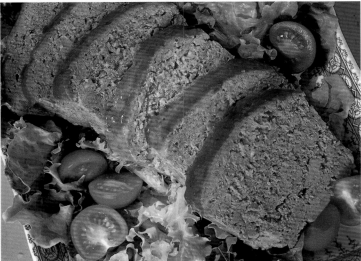

Above: Pork and Veal Pitta Burgers (page 40). Below: Stars and Stripes Barbecue Ribs

43

THE MAGIC OF MARINADES

Even the most committed meat eaters can become blasé about slabs of meat. Marinades do marvels for jaded palates and bored tastebuds. Keeping in mind a few basics, creating marinades can be a most rewarding exercise. The longer the meat marinates, the better the individual flavours will marry.

Marinades may be liquid (oil or acid-based, acting as a tenderiser), paste or dry. Dry marinades are usually a combination of salt and ground spices or dried herbs. If you don't own a blender or spice grinder, you can use your coffee grinder (wiping it out well before and after use, so your coffee tastes normal), or a mortar and pestle.

The popular Cajun dish of blackened fish is one example of a dry marinade. Pastes are made by adding a little oil to a mixture of spices and other concentrated flavour ingredients such as garlic or chilli, allowing the mixture to adhere more easily to meat. Tenderising agents include lemon juice, vinegar, wine and yoghurt and are often combined with flavours such as pepper, rosemary, bay leaves, onion or garlic. Liquid marinades may be based on oil or sauces such as soy, Worcestershire or tomato.

The only food which will be harmed by extended marinating is seafood. Don't marinate any fish or shellfish longer than one hour. A powdery texture may result, particularly if your marinade includes an acidic ingredient. In this case, marinate no longer than half an hour. The exception is raw fish salad where the process of soaking in lemon juice turns the translucent pieces of raw fish opaque and makes their texture firm and 'semi-cooked'.

Don't be fooled into believing the only reason we marinate meat is for flavour; it's also good for tenderising cheaper cuts of meat. If you don't have time to marinate meat, brush the marinade over the meat while it is cooking to give some flavour and then serve with a flavoured butter.

If guests drop in often and you decide to have a barbecue at the last minute, you may find it a good idea to have a marinade or two on hand in the refrigerator.

Basting mixtures are combinations of ingredients brushed at regular intervals over the food being cooked. Some marinades can also be used for basting when grilling and barbecuing the food.

Remember that any marinade which contains sugar or honey (or hidden sugar such as in tomato sauce), should only be brushed over almost at the end of cooking time, or the sugar will caramelise and become very dark and bitter. The success of any barbecue meal depends on the flavours imparted to the main ingredient from the basic marinade.

Preparation of good quality marinades and allowing the food to marinate for an adequate length of time is essential to a flavoursome barbecue. Ideally, large cuts of meat and whole chickens should be marinated for some hours in the refrigerator, turning occasionally, to allow for as much penetration of flavour as possible. Cubed meats and food cut into smaller portions require less marinating time.

Allow about half a cup of marinade to 500 g meat, chicken, beef, pork, seafood or vegetables. Marinate the main ingredient and then barbecue as desired. These marinades provide a quick, easy answer when you have little time for food preparation. The type of food for which each marinade recipe is suitable is indicated.

Store Cupboard Marinade

Keep this marinade handy while cooking meat. Brush food at regular intervals while barbecuing to moisten and flavour evenly.

PREPARATION TIME:
10 minutes
MAKES *1¼ cups*
USES: *Beef and lamb*

¼ **cup red wine**
¼ **cup oil**
¼ **cup barbecue sauce**
2 **tablespoons tomato sauce**
2 **teaspoons Worcestershire sauce**
1 **teaspoon chilli sauce**
½ **teaspoon ground pepper**
½ **teaspoon dried herbs**

Combine all ingredients and use to marinate main ingredients. Use with beef and lamb.
Note: This marinade will store well in an airtight container in the refrigerator for up to one week.

Lime Marinade

This flavoured marinade can also be used as a salad dressing.

PREPARATION TIME:
10 minutes
MAKES *1¼ cups*
USES: *Quail or chicken*

½ **cup olive oil**
¾ **cup lime juice**
2 **tablespoons finely chopped coriander**
2 **teaspoons sugar**
2 **teaspoons sesame oil**

Combine all ingredients and use to marinate main ingredients. Use with quail or chicken.
Note: Use any finely chopped fresh herbs for this easy marinade.

Pineapple and Ginger Marinade

This tropically inspired marinade gives a sweet flavour and rich colour to barbecued meats. There are many honeys from which to choose; a very strongly flavoured one may tend to dominate.

PREPARATION TIME:
10 minutes
MAKES *1½ cups*
USES: *Pork, chicken or lamb*

¾ **cup pineapple juice**
¼ **cup orange juice**
¼ **cup honey**
2 **tablespoons oil**
1 **tablespoon grated fresh ginger**

Combine all ingredients and use to marinate main ingredients. Use with pork, chicken or lamb.
Note: Store this marinade in an airtight container and it will keep for three days in refrigerator.

1. Combine all ingredients.

1. Finely chop the coriander.

1. Heat measuring jug for honey.

2. Store in a screw top jar.

2. Whisk all ingredients together.

2. Combine ingredients, whisk.

White Wine and Herb Marinade

This is a marinade suitable for a number of foods. Simply use a variety of fresh herbs to complement the food at hand. For seafood use thyme, dill, parsley, or a combination of these. Lamb is best with mint or with rosemary. Marjoram and sage are both good with veal. Tarragon and sage are particularly good with chicken. Marjoram, parsley and thyme go well with poultry.

PREPARATION TIME:
10 minutes
MAKES *1½ cups*
USES: *Lamb, veal, chicken, seafood*

1 cup dry white wine
½ cup olive oil
¼ cup lemon juice
¼ teaspoon ground white pepper
2 teaspoons crushed garlic
6 spring onions, finely chopped
3 tablespoons chopped fresh herbs or
3 teaspoons dried herbs

Combine all ingredients and use with relevant main ingredients. Use leftover marinade for basting.
Note: If using dried herbs, soak briefly in 1 tablespoon boiling water and add with the liquid to the marinade.

Whisk ingredients together well.

Mediterranean Marinade

This typical Greek marinade gets its distinctive flavour from the use of wild rigano imported from Greece. It is usually available at Greek delicatessens. Lamb dishes in particular are enhanced by the robust taste.

PREPARATION TIME:
5 minutes
MAKES *1 cup*
USES: *Lamb, fish and vegetables*

¾ cup olive oil
3 tablespoons lemon juice
¼ teaspoon freshly ground pepper
1 teaspoon crushed garlic
1 teaspoon crushed, dried oregano leaves or rigano
½ teaspoon salt, or to taste

Combine all ingredients and use to marinate main ingredients. Use with lamb, fish and vegetables.
Note: If you don't have a pepper mill to crush your own black pepper, heat whole peppercorns in a dry pan and while still warm crush with a mortar and pestle. The warmth of the peppercorns makes them easy to crush and improves the flavour.

Crush peppercorns with a pestle.

Singapore Satay Marinade

This marinade is great for use with skewered meats.

PREPARATION TIME:
10 minutes
MAKES *1 cup*
USES: *Beef, pork or chicken*

rind of half lemon
1 small onion, roughly chopped
2 tablespoons soy sauce
2 tablespoons peanut oil
2 teaspoons ground coriander
1 teaspoon ground cumin
½ teaspoon ground turmeric
1 teaspoon crushed garlic
2 tablespoons peanut butter
1 tablespoon fish sauce

1 Place lemon rind, onion, soy sauce and oil into a blender. Blend until smooth.
2 Add the remaining ingredients and process to a smooth paste, adding a little water to facilitate blending. Use as required. Leftover marinade can be used as a baste during cooking.
Note: Ground coriander and cumin are available in the herb and spice sections of most supermarkets. Store in a cool place away from direct sunlight. Check every couple of weeks that the flavour and aroma are still intense. Once they fade, buy new.

Process mixture until smooth.

Korean Barbecue Marinade

Use this marinade as a base for the classic Korean dish Bulgogi. Cut meat into fine strips and marinate for at least 2 hours. Cook the meat on an oiled flat plate. Sprinkle with toasted, crushed sesame seeds.

PREPARATION TIME:
10 minutes
MAKES *½ cup*
USES: *Beef*

2 teaspoons crushed garlic
1 teaspoon grated fresh ginger
1 teaspoon oriental sesame oil
1 tablespoon toasted, crushed
sesame seeds
1 medium onion, grated
½ teaspoon ground pepper
1 teaspoon chilli powder
1 tablespoon honey
1 tablespoon soy
sauce

Combine all ingredients in a small bowl and mix well. Use as required. Use any leftover marinade for basting.
Note: Toasted and crushed sesame seeds, gives that uniquely nutty flavour to the finished dish. For best results, crush the freshly toasted seeds in a mortar and pestle. Because of the oil content, sesame seeds have a tendency to turn rancid in hot weather. Buy little and often.

Combine ingredients, mix well.

Honey and Soy Marinade

A quick and easy marinade that is ideal for use in a whole range of oriental dishes. For an extra dash of flavour, try adding a little fresh ginger juice (instructions on how to make this are given in the Note below) or green ginger wine to the marinade ingredients.

PREPARATION TIME:
8 minutes
MAKES *¾ cup*
USES: *Chicken, beef and seafood*

3 tablespoons soy
sauce
1 teaspoon crushed garlic
½ teaspoon white pepper
3 tablespoons honey
3 tablespoons water

Combine all ingredients, stirring until honey is dissolved. Use as marinade, and also for basting when barbecuing.
Note: Do not use a strong, distinctively flavoured honey for this marinade as the flavour should be a balanced blend of sweet, salty and subtly spicy. For ginger juice, grate a small piece of fresh ginger and press it firmly with a teaspoon to obtain the juice.

Stir, until honey dissolves.

Teriyaki Marinade

Use this marinade when you choose Japanese-style food for your barbecue. Marinate cubes of chicken breast fillets and skewer them before barbecuing. Serve with a little extra teriyaki sauce for dipping. Soy beans are one of the ingredients in teriyaki sauce. They are the richest natural vegetable food in the world and have been grown for over 2000 years. Many Asian condiments include the soy bean.

PREPARATION TIME:
10 minutes
MAKES *1 cup*
USES: *Beef, chicken*

2 teaspoons crushed garlic
2 teaspoons sugar
½ teaspoon grated fresh ginger
4 tablespoons teriyaki sauce
(see Note)
6 tablespoons mirin or
dry sherry

Crush the garlic finely with the sugar, using the broad side of a knife on a wooden board. Combine with the grated ginger, teriyaki sauce and mirin or sherry. Use as required.
Note: Teriyaki sauce is a barbecue marinade and sauce, based on soy beans, wine, vinegar and other spices. It is readily available from most supermarkets, delicatessens.

Crush garlic finely with sugar.

Delectable Poultry

THERE IS A FABULOUS choice of poultry cuts available to use on the barbecue – chicken thigh and breast fillets, Maryland, wings and drumsticks. These poultry cuts are all there for the selective barbecue chef.

Quail, small and tender, are also ideal for outdoor cooking; allow at least one bird for each person.

These days many butchers, delicatessens and poultry specialists sell marinated chicken pieces, kebabs and other seasoned joints ready to cook. It is easy to arrive home with the makings of a wonderful barbecue meal. Simply add your own sauces and serve with fresh salads and breads.

Above: Mango Chicken (page 50). Below: Garlic and Ginger Chicken (page 51)

Place the chicken breasts skin side down onto a board and flatten out.

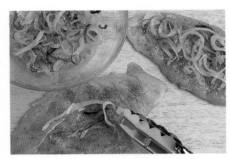

Spread equal portions of the cooked onions over each chicken breast fillet.

Place mango on chicken fillets, fold in half and secure with toothpicks.

Combine glaze ingredients in a pan. Heat and stir until thickened.

Apricot Chicken
Barbecue seasoned chicken breast fillets until golden and tender. Serve with an apricot sauce. To make sauce: Heat 1 cup apricot nectar and 1 tablespoon fruit chutney in a small pan, add a tablespoon of brandy, pepper to taste and stir in 2 teaspoons cornflour mixed with a little cold water. The sauce is ready as soon as it boils and thickens.

Mango Chicken

Don't hesitate to use fresh mangoes which need not even be completely ripe. Buy those that are firm to soft. They may be green, yellow, or bright orange with a rosy blush depending upon the variety.

PREPARATION TIME: *20 minutes*
COOKING TIME: *30 minutes*
SERVES 6

2 onions
2 tablespoons oil
1 clove garlic, crushed
6 chicken breast fillets
salt and pepper, to taste
3 medium nearly ripe mangoes
or 1 x 425 g can mangoes
watercress, to garnish

GLAZE
½ cup reserved mango juice
or purée from fresh mangoes
1 tablespoon honey
2 teaspoons chicken stock powder
1 clove garlic, crushed
1 teaspoon cornflour
cold water

1 Finely slice the onions. Heat the oil and cook onions and garlic over a low heat until golden brown. Remove from heat.
2 Place the chicken breasts skin side down onto a board or work surface. Flatten each fillet out to enclose filling. Season each with salt and pepper to taste. Place equal portions of the onion and garlic over the surface of the chicken breast fillets.
3 Drain the mango and reserve the juice for the glaze. If using fresh mangoes you must peel the fruit and cut close to the sides of the seed to get two full slices from each mango. Slice off the remaining flesh and purée in a blender.
4 Arrange mango slices on chicken breasts. Fold the chicken breast over to enclose the mango slices and onions. Secure with toothpicks or metal skewers.
5 To make Glaze: Combine mango purée or juice, honey, chicken stock powder and garlic in a small pan, cook over low heat until thoroughly combined. Add cornflour mixed smoothly with a tablespoon of cold water to the glaze. Stir over a low heat until thickened.

6 Cook chicken on a lightly oiled barbecue flat plate over medium heat for 15 minutes. Turn and cook for a further 10 minutes or until chicken is done. Brush with the glaze during last few minutes of cooking. Serve with remaining sauce on a platter garnished with watercress.

Garlic and Ginger Chicken

Garlic is healthy! It lowers blood cholesterol and aids digestion at the same time. This is an adventurous recipe to share with your friends. Best cooked on a kettle rotisserie barbecue.

PREPARATION TIME: *15 minutes +*
30 minutes marinating
COOKING TIME: *50 minutes*
SERVES 6-8

1 x 1.4 kg chicken

MARINADE
¼ cup lemon juice
¼ cup olive oil
1 tablespoon grated fresh ginger
2 cloves garlic, crushed
2 teaspoons mild curry powder
salt and pepper, to taste

GARLIC SAUCE
2 cloves garlic, crushed
¾ cup mayonnaise
1 teaspoon mild curry powder
½ teaspoon white pepper

1 Rinse the chicken, pat dry with absorbent paper. Place on a tray.
2 To make Marinade: Combine all the ingredients in a bowl and pour over the chicken. Allow to marinate for 30 minutes or overnight in the refrigerator
3 To make Garlic Sauce: Combine all the ingredients and store covered in the refrigerator until required.
4 Preheat the barbecue. Remove the chicken from the marinade and skewer onto rotisserie. Cook the chicken for approximately 50 minutes on the rotisserie. The chicken should be tender within and crisp golden brown on the outside. Serve immediately with Garlic Sauce.

Chicken Burgers

If you have a food processor, you will probably get a higher quality product mincing the chicken yourself.

PREPARATION TIME: *10 minutes*
COOKING TIME: *16 minutes*
MAKES 8

750 g minced chicken
¾ cup fresh breadcrumbs
2 teaspoons onion powder
3 teaspoons chicken stock powder
2 teaspoons garlic powder
¼ teaspoon ground dried rosemary
¼ teaspoon ground dried oregano
or thyme
¼ teaspoon white pepper
2 tablespoons white wine or hot water

1 Place chicken mince and breadcrumbs in a large bowl. Combine remaining ingredients in a small bowl, sprinkle over the chicken mince and mix well.
2 Form the mixture into eight burgers about 1.5 cm thick.
3 Cook on greased flat plate over low heat for 6-8 minutes on each side or until cooked through. Serve between sliced warmed hamburger buns, with a mixed salad and herbed butter.

To avoid whole poultry or joints becoming dry and stringy on the barbecue or staying bloody near the bone, do not cook too quickly – slow, indirect cooking gives the best results.

Chicken Burgers

**Coconut
Chicken Parcels**
Combine ½ cup
canned coconut milk,
½ teaspoon ground
turmeric, salt,
ground pepper,
1 small chopped
onion and
½ teaspoon crushed
garlic. Place chicken
thigh fillets on
squares of baking
paper and double
foil. Top with a
spoonful of the
coconut mixture,
bring foil up and fold
to seal, making sure
to keep the seal on
top. Barbecue for
10-15 minutes and
serve with steamed
rice.

Chicken Satay

This favourite is sure to please the hungry hordes. Chicken satay can also be served as an entrée course.

PREPARATION TIME: *15 minutes +*
1 hour marinating
COOKING TIME: *6 minutes*
SERVES 6

**500 g skinless chicken breast or
thigh fillets**

MARINADE AND SAUCE
1 large onion, grated
2 tablespoons lemon or lime juice
2 cloves garlic, crushed
2 teaspoons grated fresh ginger
**2 teaspoons sambal olek or
crushed chillies**
⅓ cup soy sauce
2 tablespoons brown sugar
1 tablespoon sesame oil
¾ cup coconut milk
½ cup crunchy peanut butter
2 tablespoons toasted sesame seeds

1 Cut the chicken breasts into bite-sized squares. Combine onion, lemon juice, garlic, ginger, sambal olek, soy sauce, brown sugar and sesame oil. Pour over the prepared chicken and stir to coat all the pieces thoroughly. Allow to marinate for 1 hour in the refrigerator. Meanwhile, soak the bamboo skewers in cold water.
2 Remove the chicken pieces from the marinade and thread onto twelve soaked bamboo skewers, leaving a portion of the skewer free for handling. Barbecue over preheated grill for about 6 minutes, turning until they are nicely browned. Brush with a little extra oil if necessary.
3 Pour the remaining marinade into a pan and place on the edge of the barbecue. Add the coconut milk and peanut butter, stir until the mixture boils and thickens. Serve satays on a platter, sprinkled with sesame seeds. Accompany with steamed rice and serve with satay sauce.

Spicy Chicken Wings

Chicken wings are such delectable morsels, the flesh succulent and the skin meltingly crisp. No wonder everyone loves eating them in many ways and with many added flavours. This recipe is a mildly spiced version.

PREPARATION TIME: *10 minutes +*
1 hour marinating
COOKING TIME: *20-25 minutes*
SERVES 6

1.5 kg (about 12) chicken wings
6 teaspoons mild curry powder
2 cloves garlic, crushed
1 tablespoon oil
2 tablespoons lemon juice
½ teaspoon white pepper
¼ cup water
**1 tablespoon chicken stock
powder**

1 Remove the tips from the chicken wings, rinse and pat dry with absorbent paper. Score through skin and flesh with a sharp knife.
2 Combine the remaining ingredients, mixing well.
3 Pour the marinade over the prepared wings. Mix to coat well.
4 Grill over lightly oiled preheated barbecue on medium heat for 12 minutes, turn and continue cooking until tender and golden brown.

Saffron Chicken

Saffron is the world's most expensive spice and has a wonderful flavour. But be warned, it has many imitations both in powder and strand form. Buy from a reputable dealer (such as a chefs' supplier) or look for a well-known brand name or you could be paying for coloured powder which delivers no flavour at all.

PREPARATION TIME: *15 minutes +*
30 minutes marinating
COOKING TIME: *25 minutes*
SERVES 8

8 chicken breast fillets

MARINADE
1/4 teaspoon saffron
powder (see Note)
2 tablespoons hot water
1 tablespoon lime juice
1 teaspoon ground sweet paprika
1/2 teaspoon ground pepper
1 clove garlic, crushed
2 tablespoons olive oil
1 teaspoon onion powder
3 teaspoons chicken stock powder
1/4 cup sour cream
1 teaspoon cornflour
1/2 cup milk

1 Lightly score the chicken breast fillets, criss-cross and pat dry with absorbent paper. Place in a shallow dish. Dissolve the saffron in the hot water and combine with the lime juice, paprika, pepper, garlic, olive oil and onion powder.

2 Pour over the chicken and turn to coat in the marinade. Allow chicken to stand for 30 minutes.

3 Remove the chicken from the marinade. Cook chicken on preheated flat plate over low heat for 8-10 minutes each side, or until the chicken is tender and golden, turning once during the cooking.

4 Place remaining marinade in a small pan with chicken stock powder and sour cream. Combine cornflour and milk, stir into the sauce and heat until thickened. Season to taste with pepper. Serve this sauce with the chicken.

Note: If purchasing saffron strands (most brands are sold in strand form) lightly toast half a teaspoon of the strands in a dry pan, shaking the pan to prevent burning. Empty onto a small saucer and when cool and crisp, crush with the back of a spoon.

Above: Saffron Chicken
Below: Chicken Satay
Right: Spicy Chicken

Chicken and Prawn Kebabs

This diet-conscious barbecue fare does away with the need for a marinade which may include oil. Wrap cubes of boned and skinned chicken and diced fresh or frozen vegetables in foil bundles, first sprinkling with herbs and a little lemon juice. Cook directly on the barbecue for 8-10 minutes or until chicken and vegetables are tender. Use double industrial strength foil.

Surf 'n' turf is what the famous combination of lobster and steak is named in America. This recipe is a less expensive version, it features seafood and chicken – a farmyard product.

PREPARATION TIME: *25 minutes +*
30 minutes marinating
COOKING TIME: *20 minutes*
SERVES 6

350 g chicken breast fillets
500 g large green prawns
1 x 425 g can apricot halves,
in natural juice
1 x 440 g can pineapple rings
2 teaspoons grated fresh ginger
2 tablespoons olive oil
salt and white pepper, to taste
2 teaspoons cornflour
1 tablespoon water
1 teaspoon grated fresh ginger, extra
2 spring onions, finely sliced

1 Cut the chicken into large pieces. Peel and devein the prawns. Drain the apricot halves and pineapple slices, reserving the juice. Cut the pineapple slices into four. Thread the prepared chicken, prawns and fruit alternately onto soaked bamboo or metal skewers.
2 Combine 1 cup reserved pineapple juice with grated ginger, olive oil, salt and pepper. Pour over the kebabs and allow to marinate for 30 minutes.
3 Remove from the marinade and barbecue over a hot flat plate for 5 minutes each side or until the chicken is tender and prawns have turned pink. Meanwhile, heat remaining marinade in a pan on the edge of the barbecue, thicken with combined cornflour and water, add the extra grated ginger and spring onions and allow to boil until the sauce thickens. Serve Chicken and Prawn Kebabs immediately.

Barbecued Quail with Garlic and Sour Cream

These small birds make good eating, especially when well cooked over a barbecue. The garlic in this recipe is the whole head, cooked until sweet and mellow. Spread it on toast for a new taste sensation.

PREPARATION TIME: *15 minutes +*
30 minutes marinating
COOKING TIME: *40 minutes*
SERVES 6

12 quail

MARINADE
6 tablespoons olive oil
1/3 cup dry white wine
1/3 cup finely chopped spring onions
1/2 cup chopped fresh herbs
2 cloves garlic, crushed
6 whole heads of garlic

SOUR CREAM SAUCE
1 cup sour cream
2 tablespoons finely chopped
spring onions
salt and white pepper, to taste
little lime or lemon juice, to taste

1 Place the quail on a board breast side down. Cut through the back with poultry shears to butterfly and discard backbone.
2 To make Marinade: Combine olive oil, white wine, spring onions, fresh herbs and garlic. Pour over the quail and allow to marinate for 30 minutes.
3 Wrap the garlic heads in a double layer of industrial-strength foil.
4 Place the wrapped garlic directly into the coals – not flames – of the fire or place on top of the grill. Cook for 30-40 minutes. This long, slow cooking mellows the flavour of the garlic.
5 Remove the quail from the marinade and barbecue on a lightly oiled grill for 12-15 minutes. Turn occasionally and brush with the marinade during cooking.
6 To make Sour Cream Sauce: Combine the sour cream, and spring onions and season with salt and pepper, and juice to taste. Serve the barbecued quail with knobs of garlic and Sour Cream Sauce.

Clockwise: Barbecued Quail with Garlic & Sour Cream, Chicken & Prawn Kebabs, Chicken Maryland (page 56)

Honey Soy Chicken Drumsticks

Removing skin from chicken cuts down on fat, but since the protective covering is no longer there, take special care to cook gently to avoid flesh drying out.

Just the dish to introduce spicy flavours to first timers. Add a little chilli sauce for those who prefer it hotter. Best cooked on a kettle barbecue.

PREPARATION TIME: *15 minutes +*
1 hour marinating
COOKING TIME: *25-30 minutes*
SERVES 6

⅓ cup soy sauce
2 cloves garlic, crushed
1 small onion, grated
½ teaspoon white pepper
1 tablespoon honey
¼ cup green ginger wine
12 (1.5 kg) chicken drumsticks

1 Combine the soy sauce, garlic, onion, pepper, honey and green ginger wine in a small pan, stir over a low heat until the honey softens and the ingredients are thoroughly mixed.
2 Remove the skin from the drumsticks and score through the flesh at 2 cm intervals. Pour the marinade over the prepared chicken and allow to marinate for 1 hour.

Honey Soy Chicken
Drumsticks

3 Remove drumsticks from the marinade and barbecue over preheated, oiled flat plate with the hood down for 20-25 minutes, turning occasionally until the chicken is tender and juices are clear. Brush two or three times with remaining marinade towards end of cooking. Serve with salad.
Note: If using an open barbecue, allow extra time for cooking.

Chicken Maryland

This may not be the original Chicken Maryland (crumbed and deep fried) but it features the whole leg portions which have come to be known by this name. This recipe is most suitable for barbecuing.

PREPARATION TIME: *20 minutes +*
30 minutes marinating
COOKING TIME: *30 minutes*
SERVES 6

1 x 440 g can pineapple slices
6 Chicken Maryland pieces

MARINADE
2 tablespoons oil
½ cup tomato sauce
1 tablespoon malt vinegar
1 tablespoon barbecue sauce
1 tablespoon brown sugar
¼ cup reserved pineapple juice
1 clove garlic, crushed
salt and pepper, to taste

1 Drain the pineapple slices and reserve the juice.
2 To make marinade: Combine oil, tomato sauce, vinegar, barbecue sauce, sugar, pineapple juice, garlic, salt and pepper in a small pan over low heat. Brush the marinade over the surface of the chicken and allow to marinate for 30 minutes, or longer in the refrigerator if a stronger flavour is required.
3 Remove the chicken and cook over preheated lightly oiled barbecue flat plate for 30-35 minutes or until tender and juices run clear. Turn often and brush with remaining marinade towards end of cooking. Cook the pineapple rings along with the chicken during the last 5 minutes, brushing with the marinade.

Kashmiri Chicken Roast

This larger chicken needs enclosed cooking to be done well and is best cooked on a kettle rotisserie barbecue.

PREPARATION TIME: *20 minutes +*
30 minutes marinating
COOKING TIME: *1 hour 10 minutes*
SERVES 4 - 6

1 x 1.4 kg chicken

MARINADE
¼ teaspoon ground saffron
2 tablespoons hot water
2 teaspoons ground fenugreek leaves
2 cloves garlic, crushed
1 teaspoon grated fresh ginger
½ teaspoon chilli powder
2 teaspoons garam masala
½ teaspoon turmeric
½ teaspoon ground pepper
3 tablespoons blanched almonds
or ¼ cup ground almonds
½ cup chopped fresh coriander
1 tablespoon ghee or unsalted butter
½ cup warm water

1 Remove the skin from the chicken and lightly score the flesh criss-cross fashion.
2 To make Marinade: Dissolve saffron in hot water and combine with the remaining ingredients. Use the marinade to coat the entire chicken, both inside and out. Place onto a rotisserie bar.
3 Heat kettle barbecue to high, arrange the skewered chicken in place and roast for 20 minutes.
4 Lower the heat to medium and cook further 30 minutes. Baste the chicken with remaining marinade. Raise the heat and cook a final 10 minutes. Stand covered for 10 minutes before carving. Serve with salad and flat bread, chapatis or naan.
Note: Chicken can be roasted in a conventional oven with good results. Stand marinated chicken on a rack in a baking dish, add 1 cup of water to baking dish. Cook in a moderately high oven 190°C for 20 minutes, reduce heat to moderate 180°C and cook a further 40 minutes. Allow the chicken to stand covered 10 minutes before carving.

Kashmiri Chicken Roast

Chicken with Orange and Mustard Glaze

Be careful not to overcook the chicken breasts as they will toughen. For the best results, use the touch test.

PREPARATION TIME: *15 minutes*
COOKING TIME: *15 minutes*
SERVES 8

8 chicken breast halves on the bone
salt and pepper, to taste

SAUCE
½ cup chicken stock
¾ cup marmalade
1 tablespoon seeded mustard
1 tablespoon French mustard

1 Trim the chicken breasts and pat dry with absorbent paper. Season lightly with salt and pepper on both sides.
2 To make Sauce: Place all ingredients in a small pan and place on the barbecue flat plate to heat through.
3 Cook the chicken breasts over a hot, oiled flat plate for 10-15 minutes, brushing with a little sauce from time to time during the last 5 minutes of cooking.
4 Serve the remaining sauce with the cooked chicken.

Cook chicken pieces or halved chickens with the bone and flesh towards the heat first. Then, when cooking is more than half way through, turn and cook the skin side.

Wrap par-boiled chicken legs in trimmed bacon rashers and secure with toothpicks. Finish cooking on the barbecue over indirect heat until chicken is tender and bacon crisp. Sprinkle with a few drops of Worcestershire or chilli sauce before serving.

Thai Thigh Fillets

Thai Thigh Fillets

Chicken breast fillets can also be used for this spicy recipe.

PREPARATION TIME: *15 minutes +*
1 hour marinating
COOKING TIME: *12 minutes*
SERVES 6

500 g skinless chicken thigh fillets

MARINADE
3 tablespoons pepper coriander paste
(see Note)
1 clove garlic, crushed
½ teaspoon turmeric
½ teaspoon chilli powder or to taste
1 tablespoon water
2 teaspoons chicken stock powder
1 tablespoon peanut oil

1 Cut each thigh in half, lightly score criss-cross and set aside.
2 To make Marinade: Combine all the ingredients, mix well and marinate chicken for 1 hour or longer in the refrigerator.
3 Heat barbecue flat plate and place the chicken pieces on the flat plate, grilling them 6 minutes each side, or until done to your liking. Serve with salad.

Note: Pepper Coriander Paste: Pound, in mortar and pestle, 3 tablespoons chopped fresh coriander, 2 cloves garlic and 1 teaspoon whole black peppercorns.

Indonesian Chicken

This recipe was cooked in a wok or covered gas barbecue, but can be adapted to any barbecue if the initial marinating and par-cooking is done ahead, leaving the final cooking to be done over the coals.

PREPARATION TIME: *20 minutes +*
1 hour marinating
COOKING TIME: *45 minutes*
SERVES 6-8

1 x 1.4 kg chicken

MARINADE
2 cloves garlic, crushed
1 medium onion, chopped
1 teaspoon chopped fresh ginger
3 red chillies, chopped
1 teaspoon turmeric
salt and pepper, to taste
1 teaspoon grated lemon rind
1 teaspoon ground coriander
½ cup coconut milk
4 lime leaves
1 tablespoon brown sugar
2 tablespoons white vinegar
1½ cups coconut milk, extra
1 cup water

1 Split the chicken in half, through the breastbone and down the back and remove the backbone.
2 To make Marinade: Blend garlic, onion, ginger, chillies, turmeric, salt, pepper, lemon rind, coriander and coconut milk. Marinate the chicken with the mixture for 1 hour and remove.
3 In a wok, heat remaining marinade, lime leaves, brown sugar, vinegar, coconut milk and water. Cook for 2-3 minutes. Add the marinated chicken and simmer for 15 minutes, basting while cooking. Turn over and cook another 15 minutes.
4 Remove chicken from the wok. Place on a barbecue and cook until browned and firm to the touch.
5 Serve the remaining marinade as a sauce. Sprinkle with chopped coriander.

Above: Chicken with Orange and Mustard Glaze (page 57). Below: Indonesian Chicken

Take care not to overcook chicken, especially breasts as they are inclined to be a dry meat and can be tough and fibrous if not properly cooked.

Left: Chicken Koftas
Right: Garlic Chicken

Garlic Chicken

A few soaked mesquite or hickory chips can be added to the fire to give the chicken a delicious smoky flavour.

PREPARATION TIME: *10 minutes +*
1 hour marinating
COOKING TIME: *5-10 minutes*
SERVES *8*

8 chicken breast fillets
⅓ cup olive oil
6 cloves garlic, crushed
salt and pepper, to taste

1 Trim all visible fat from fillets, dry and score the smooth surface lightly. In a baking dish, combine oil, garlic and seasonings. Add fillets one at a time, spoon over the garlic oil. Cover and refrigerate overnight, or allow to marinate at room temperature for 1 hour.
2 Heat barbecue grill plate and cook chicken over a medium heat until firm to the touch.

Chicken Koftas

A simple preparation, the pepper and coriander giving it a hint of Thai flavour.

PREPARATION TIME: *20 minutes*
COOKING TIME: *8 minutes*
SERVES *8*

500 g minced chicken
3 tablespoons pepper coriander paste
(see Note – Chicken Reuben page 61)
1 egg, lightly beaten
1 clove garlic, crushed
1 teaspoon salt
1 cup cornflake crumbs
2 teaspoons chilli sauce

1 Mix all ingredients together and form into eight long koftas (torpedo shapes) on flat metal skewers or bamboo skewers.
2 Place on rack over heated barbecue. Cover and cook 8 minutes, turning frequently to avoid charring. Cook to golden brown and serve between hot split torpedo rolls with salad and rich tomato sauce.

Chicken Reuben

This is a marvellous blending of flavours from many Asian lands, with scant regard for boundaries. Forget purism, enjoy this delectable creation.

PREPARATION TIME: *20 minutes +*
1 hour marinating
COOKING TIME: *10 minutes*
SERVES 6

1 tablespoon pepper coriander paste
(see Note)
1 clove garlic, crushed
1 teaspoon grated fresh ginger
2 teaspoons curry powder
¼ teaspoon citric acid
¼ cup water
2 teaspoons chicken stock powder
1 tablespoon peanut oil
¼ teaspoon salt
1 teaspoon garam masala
500 g skinless chicken thigh fillets

1 Mix together pepper coriander paste, garlic, ginger, curry powder, citric acid, water, chicken stock powder, peanut oil, salt and garam masala.
2 Lightly score the chicken, in criss-cross fashion. Place the chicken fillets in the prepared marinade and marinate for about 1 hour or refrigerate overnight.
3 Preheat barbecue and cook chicken 10 minutes over medium heat turning once, until chicken is done. Eat with steamed rice or flat bread and a salad.
Note: To make Pepper Coriander Paste: Pound, in mortar and pestle, 3 tablespoons chopped fresh coriander, 2 cloves garlic and 1 teaspoon whole black peppercorns. Steamed rice is a great accompaniment to Asian-style barbecue dishes. To cook by the absorption method, place 2 cups long grain rice in a pan, add 3 cups water and a teaspoon of salt. Bring to the boil, cover, reduce heat and simmer on lowest heat for 15 minutes. Fluff with a fork and serve. Sufficient for 4-6 people.

Chicken Reuben

One of the quickest and simplest barbecue ideas has got to be chicken fillets (minus skin) coated in oil and ground pepper – like pepper steaks. Don't cook too long or they will dry out. Serve with a flavoured butter.

Succulent Shellfish & Seafood

THERE ARE NUMEROUS delicious ways to barbecue seafood. Depending on the variety and size, it may be wrapped in baking paper and char-grilled, cooked in a fish basket, marinated and tossed on the barbecue or skewered as kebabs.

When barbecuing fish on an electric or gas barbecue, a medium-high heat is required. Always remember that cooking times are approximate so use your judgement. Be careful to avoid burning fish. Overcooking shellfish will cause it to shrink and toughen. If you are cooking over an open charcoal grill, cook over glowing coals, not over flames and grease the barbecue plate before cooking, so that the seafood doesn't stick.

Clockwise from top: Barbecued Lobster, Blackened Fish Fillets, Chilli Scallops and Prawn Kebabs (all recipes page 64)

Blackened Fish Fillets

For the best results when barbecuing choose firm white fish fillets which are of an even thickness of about 1 cm.

PREPARATION TIME: *10 minutes +*
30 minutes marinating
COOKING TIME: *5 minutes*
SERVES *4*

4 medium firm white fish fillets

SEASONING MIXTURE
2 tablespoons ground black pepper
3 teaspoons garlic powder
3 teaspoons onion powder
1 tablespoon dried thyme
1 teaspoon salt
3 teaspoons hot chilli powder
1 tablespoon plain flour
2 teaspoons ground dried oregano
Tabasco sauce to taste

¼ cup olive oil or ghee

1 Pat fish fillets dry with absorbent paper. To make Seasoning Mixture: Combine all ingredients and use to coat fish. Allow to stand for 30 minutes.
2 Heat flat plate of open barbecue. Spread the surface with olive oil or ghee.
3 Cook fillets approximately 4-5 minutes each side turning only once.

Barbecued Lobster

The price of lobster being what it is, this is the most expensive recipe in the book but one of the most enjoyable.

PREPARATION TIME: *20 minutes*
COOKING TIME: *5 minutes*
SERVES *6-8*

6 small green lobster tails
3 tablespoons olive oil
salt, to taste
3 tablespoons lemon juice
1 tablespoon chopped fresh dill
ground pepper, to taste
lemon wedges, to serve

1 Cut the lobster tails in half lengthwise and slit the underside of the tails with the point of a sharp knife to allow access to the flesh. Combine the olive oil, salt, lemon juice, dill and pepper to taste.
2 Brush the marinade onto the lobster flesh. (Retain the shell to protect the delicate flesh from intense heat.)
3 Barbecue the lobster on a preheated and oiled flat plate. First turn the cut side down to seal, just for a few seconds. Then use tongs to turn the pieces over and cook covered for 5 minutes or until the shells turn pink. Serve lobster with a lemony mayonnaise and a tossed green salad.

Chilli Scallops and Prawn Kebabs

This culinary creation is fiery hot. If you are not too sure about your chilli tolerance, reduce the amount of oriental chilli bean sauce.

PREPARATION TIME: *20 minutes +*
10 minutes marinating
COOKING TIME: *8 minutes*
SERVES *6-8*

1 clove garlic, crushed
1 tablespoon grated fresh ginger
2 teaspoons sesame oil
1 tablespoon oriental chilli
bean sauce (see Note)
1 tablespoon soy sauce
2 teaspoons tomato paste
1 tablespoon sugar
1 tablespoon lemon juice
1 kg large green prawns
250 g scallops

1 Combine the crushed garlic, ginger, sesame oil, chilli bean sauce, soy sauce, tomato paste, sugar and lemon juice.
2 Peel prawns and devein, leaving tails on. Clean the scallops. Add prawns and scallops to the marinade. Cover and marinate for 10-15 minutes.
3 Skewer prawns and scallops on flat metal skewers.
4 Cook on a preheated, lightly oiled barbecue flat plate or grill plate for 4 minutes each side. Baste with the remaining marinade during cooking. Serve with rice.

Purchasing fillets can be a little tricky. Often shops fillet fish left from the previous day. Look for fillets which are shiny and firm with a good shape and not discoloured. If you're not happy with the fillets on display, ask them to fillet the fish you choose. The head and bones can be used for stock.

Mustard Mayonnaise
Mix together 1 cup mayonnaise with 2 teaspoons mustard and black pepper to taste. Serve with whole fish or with fish fillets.

Note: Chilli bean sauce is an oil-based soya bean, garlic and extra hot chilli paste. Use with caution. Available from Chinese and Asian food outlets.

Firecracker Prawns

These prawns certainly have some fire, but if you really like it spicy, adjust the cayenne pepper according to your taste.

PREPARATION TIME: *15 minutes*
COOKING TIME: *8 minutes*
SERVES 6

1 kg large green prawns
2 tablespoons olive oil

DRY SPICE MIXTURE
2 teaspoons black pepper
½ teaspoon salt
1 teaspoon onion powder
1 teaspoon dried chilli flakes
1 teaspoon ground sweet paprika
½ teaspoon cayenne pepper
1 teaspoon ground dried oregano
1 teaspoon thyme
1 teaspoon garlic powder

1 Peel the prawns, leaving tails on. Skewer six prawns on eight metal skewers. Brush with olive oil.
2 To make Dry Spice Mixture: Combine ingredients and sprinkle over the prawns on both sides. Grill over a hot barbecue flat plate or grill plate for 4 minutes each side or until prawns are pink and tender. Serve with Barbecue Hollandaise Sauce (see page 96).

Thai Fish Cakes

In Bangkok we had these spicy morsels as an entrée. They were most enjoyable but not what you'd call filling. Double the quantities for a main dish.

PREPARATION TIME: *30 minutes*
COOKING TIME: *8 minutes*
SERVES 6

10 spinach leaves
250 g bream fillets
1 tablespoon fish sauce
¼ cup finely chopped spring onions
1 tablespoon finely chopped fresh coriander leaves, roots and stems
2 teaspoons grated lime rind
1 clove garlic, crushed
1 teaspoon chilli sauce
¼ teaspoon ground pepper
¼ cup thick coconut milk
1 egg

1 Blanch the spinach leaves in boiling water for 10 seconds and cool them in iced water.
2 Remove skin, any stray bones and cut fish fillets into pieces. Combine in a food processor with the remaining ingredients until the mixture is smooth. Divide the fish mixture between six spinach leaves, placing two leaves together if they are small. Roll the spinach over to enclose the fish filling. Wrap each parcel in foil.
3 Place on a preheated barbecue flat plate and cook for 4 minutes each side, turning once. Serve immediately and let each person remove the foil from their portion.
Note: The use of the roots of coriander herb in this recipe is not a mistake. It lends a stronger flavour to the dish and is used in most Thai recipes.

Shellfish should have no discolouration around the joint and be firmly closed. Shells should be lustrous and not broken in any way. They should smell of the sea.

Thai Fish Cakes

Storing whole fresh fish: If it hasn't been gutted and scaled, you will need to do this before storing. Rubbing with moist absorbent paper dipped in cooking salt can help to remove any blood from the inside cavity. Wash fillets in cold water and pat dry with absorbent paper. Wrap in plastic wrap and place in an airtight container. Store in refrigerator and use within two days.

Prawns with Lemon and Garlic

Prawns with Lemon and Garlic

Marinating prawns for too long can make them powdery, especially if the marinade contains an acid ingredient such as yoghurt, vinegar or lemon juice. Sea salt is available from good kitchen shops and leading food outlets.

PREPARATION TIME: *20 minutes +*
10 minutes marinating
COOKING TIME: *5 minutes*
SERVES 4-6

1 kg large green prawns
¼ cup olive oil
1 tablespoon lemon juice
2 cloves garlic, crushed
2 spring onions, finely chopped
½ teaspoon sea salt
ground black pepper,
to taste
lemon quarters, to serve

1 Shell and devein prawns. Mix remaining ingredients in a glass or ceramic bowl and stir in prawns. Allow to marinate for 10 minutes.
2 On a flat plate over full heat toss prawns until they start to curl up and become opaque. Serve with lemon quarters and crusty white bread.

Stuffed Bream

Make sure you do not overcook the fish, which would cause the flesh to toughen and dry. When ready, the flesh should be tender and white.

PREPARATION TIME: *15 minutes*
COOKING TIME: *20 minutes*
SERVES 4

1 large bream, gutted and scaled

FILLING
1 cup fresh breadcrumbs
2 tablespoons chopped fresh parsley
1 tablespoon chopped fresh thyme
1 lemon
½ teaspoon salt
½ teaspoon white pepper
15 g butter, melted
2 tablespoons olive oil
wedges of lemon, to serve

1 Clean the inside cavity of the fish with absorbent paper dipped in coarse salt. Score both sides of the fish at 2 cm intervals with a sharp knife.
2 To make Filling: Place breadcrumbs, parsley and thyme in a small bowl. Finely grate the rind of the lemon, squeeze and strain juice. Add to the breadcrumbs with salt, pepper and melted butter, mix well.
3 Fill the fish cavity with the prepared filling and secure with small metal skewers. Brush the outside with a little olive oil.
4 Place the fish in a fish frame or grill plate and barbecue over a lightly oiled flat plate for 15-20 minutes, turning once, or until cooked. Serve with wedges of lemon.
Note: A fisheroo or fish frame is obtained from barbecue or camping accessory outlets. Fish can also be cooked in a well greased foil parcel of double thickness.
Thyme can be used fresh or dried, it is a herb that improves with drying.

Left: Firecracker Prawns (page 65). Right: Stuffed Bream

Seafood and Vegetable Parcels

These tasty parcels are almost a meal on their own. Serve them with steamed rice or tossed salad.

PREPARATION TIME: *15 minutes*
COOKING TIME: *15 minutes*
SERVES *4*

4 small bream fillets
12 large green prawns, shelled and de-veined
8 scallops
1 red capsicum, cut into strips
2 small carrots, cut into strips
2 small zucchini, cut in to strips

MARINADE
½ cup chopped fresh coriander
2 tablespoons finely chopped spring onions
½ teaspoon grated fresh ginger
2 tablespoons white wine
1 tablespoon olive oil
1 teaspoon lemon pepper
2 tablespoons water
2 teaspoons chicken stock powder

Thin fillets of white fish can be cooked on the barbecue flat plate either side for a short time until opaque. A whole fish may be wrapped in baking paper or banana leaves, then in heavy-duty foil and cooked on indirect heat of the barbecue for a longer period. Protected in this way, it will retain its juices and flavour.

Trout can be seasoned, wrapped in baking paper and heavy-duty foil and barbecued on the outer ends of the char-grill. Being a delicate fish it should be cooked in a fish basket or frame on a covered barbecue.

1   Prepare four sheets of double foil about 30 cm square. Top each square of foil with a piece of baking paper about the same size. Place a fish fillet on each square. Place three prawns and two cleaned scallops on each fish fillet.
2   Blanch the vegetables for 1 minute in boiling water. Drain and divide evenly between the parcels.
3   To make Marinade: Combine all the ingredients and spoon over the seafood and vegetables. Bring the paper over the top of the seafood and fold tightly to make an enclosed parcel. Wrap the foil over the paper to enclose and strengthen the parcel. Place on a baking tray.
4   Cook on a preheated moderately hot barbecue plate for approximately 15 minutes.
Note: Be careful not to overcook the seafood parcels, as the seafood will become tough very quickly. These parcels can also be cooked in a moderate oven 180°C for about 15 minutes.

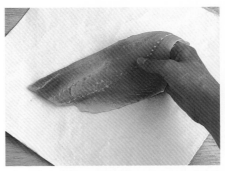

Place fish fillets on baking paper and foil squares measuring about 30 cm square.

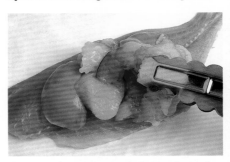

Arrange three prawns and two cleaned scallops over each fish fillet.

Blanch vegetables, drain well and divide vegetables evenly between the parcels.

Prepare marinade, spoon over seafood and vegetable parcels. Seal tightly.

Chilli Garlic Prawns

Serve these prawns in miniature cast-iron pots or heat-proof ramekins. If you don't have them, make the full quantity in a large, heavy-based cast-iron frying pan and let the guests help themselves.

PREPARATION TIME: *15 minutes*
COOKING TIME: *3 minutes*
SERVES 6

1 kg large green prawns

CHILLI-GARLIC OIL
⅔ cup olive oil
90 g butter, melted
4 cloves garlic, crushed
2 teaspoons finely chopped red chillies
½ teaspoon ground black pepper
salt, to taste

1 Peel and de-vein the prawns, slit them through the back to butterfly. Heat six cast-iron pots on a preheated barbecue flat plate.
2 To make Chilli Garlic Oil: Combine the remaining ingredients and heat until bubbling hot in a heavy frying pan. Add the prawns and toss until they are coated with the mixture.
3 Divide the garlic mixture between the pots and cook until the prawns curl and turn pink, about 2 or 3 minutes.
4 Serve immediately with crusty bread.
Note: When preparing fresh chillies it is essential that you wear disposable gloves. Don't touch your face or body. If preferred you can buy prepared chillies in bottles (sambal olek) at Asian stores.

Left: Seafood and Vegetable Parcels. Right: Chilli Garlic Prawns

When using foil to package foods which have an acid ingredient, line the foil with a layer of baking paper to prevent any undesirable reactions.

Barbecued Scallops

Scallops have become increasingly expensive over the last few years. This dish you can simply serve as a entrée and allow your guests just a taste of the tempting morsels. Serve with steamed rice and accompany with a little chilli sauce if desired.

PREPARATION TIME: *15 minutes +*
15 minutes marinating
COOKING TIME: *5 minutes*
SERVES 4-6

500 g scallops
2 tablespoons olive oil
1 clove garlic, crushed
2 spring onions,
finely shredded
salt and pepper, to taste

Mint Dressing
Blend until combined, 1/2 cup sour cream, 1/2 cup yoghurt, 2 tablespoons chopped fresh mint, 1 clove garlic, crushed and salt to taste. Serve with chilled seafoods.

Barbecued Scallops

1 Rinse scallops, removing any visible veins of dirt. Mix together remaining ingredients and stir in scallops. Marinate for 15 minutes in the refrigerator.
2 Cook over a moderately hot flat plate or at the edge of the barbecue where the heat is not too fierce, until they turn white. Do not overcook or they will toughen.
Note: Scallops require a short cooking time. They can easily become tough and rubbery with excess cooking so wait until your guests are ready before you cook them. If you are using scallops which have been frozen, allow them to defrost completely in the refrigerator and drain well before marinating.

Barbecued Spiced Fish

Choose white fish fillets for this recipe so that the unique flavours of the marinade are not masked by a strong flavoured fish.

PREPARATION TIME: *15 minutes*
COOKING TIME: *20 minutes*
SERVES 4

4 large, firm white fish fillets
60 g butter, melted

DRY MARINADE
1/2 teaspoon salt
2 teaspoons ground sweet paprika
1/2 teaspoon white pepper
1/2 teaspoon ground cayenne
1/4 teaspoon ground dried oregano
1/4 teaspoon dried basil
1/4 teaspoon dried thyme
1 teaspoon garlic powder
1 teaspoon onion powder

1 Dry fish fillets with absorbent paper and brush with melted butter, set aside.
2 To make Dry Marinade: Combine all the dry spices and sprinkle over the buttered fish fillets.
3 Barbecue fillets on a lightly oiled flat plate for 8-10 minutes, turning once during the cooking time.
Note: You may find it easier to make a double quantity of this dry marinade and store the remaining mixture for later use. Store in a covered airtight jar in the freezer for best results. It adds flavour to seafood, poultry and beef.

Above: Barbecued Spiced Fish. Below: Prawn Burgers (page 72)

Prawn Burgers

A delicious burger variation to serve for special-occasions.

PREPARATION TIME: *15 minutes*
COOKING TIME: *4 minutes*
SERVES 6

500 g large green prawns, shelled and
deveined
1 egg, lightly beaten
1 tablespoon dry sherry
1 teaspoon grated fresh ginger
1 clove garlic, crushed
2 tablespoons cornflour
3 tablespoons finely chopped spring
onions
2 tablespoons finely chopped water
chestnuts
½ cup cornflake crumbs
salt, to taste
3 tablespoons oil

SAUCE
2 teaspoons Worcestershire sauce
1 tablespoon white wine vinegar
2 tablespoons water
2 teaspoons sugar
1 teaspoon grated fresh ginger
Tabasco sauce, to taste

lime wedges, to serve
6 hamburger buns, to serve

1 Finely chop prawns, combine with eggs, sherry, ginger, garlic, cornflour, spring onions, water chestnuts and cornflake crumbs. Mix well. Season to taste.
2 To make Sauce: Combine ingredients in a small bowl.
3 Heat barbecue flat plate to medium hot and spread with oil. Divide prawn mixture evenly into six portions and cook in egg rings brushed with oil. Cook for 2 minutes on each side or until set and firm. Do not overcook. Serve Prawn Burgers with combined sauce ingredients, lime wedges and hamburger buns.
Note: Serve with a crisp salad.

Calamari Rings
Place calamari rings in a basin. Add 2 tablespoons green ginger wine, 2 tablespoons soy sauce, 1 teaspoon grated fresh ginger, 1 clove garlic, crushed and 1 teaspoon chopped or crushed chilli. Stir to coat, leave for 15 minutes. Toss onto an oiled barbecue flat plate and turn over high heat for 1-2 minutes or until the rings are tender and cooked. Serve immediately with rice and extra soy sauce.

Chilli Crab

Peanut oil is used in this recipe. It is unrefined and has quite a strong peanutty fragrance and flavour. Widely used in Asia and available from most Asian food outlets. We used a wok attachment for our barbecue with this recipe. Alternatively you can simply use a wok on your conventional hot plate.

PREPARATION TIME: *20 minutes*
COOKING TIME: *15 minutes*
SERVES 2-4 *as an entrée*

⅓ cup peanut oil
3 cloves garlic, crushed
2 fresh red chillies, finely chopped
1 teaspoon grated fresh ginger
1 tablespoons chilli paste or sambal olek
⅓ cup tomato sauce
2 tablespoons sugar
1 tablespoon soy sauce
1 teaspoon oriental sesame oil
3 medium-sized cooked crabs

1 Using a cleaver or a heavy-bladed sharp knife, cut crabs in half. Wash crabs under cold water, remove fibrous tissues and stomach bag.
2 Heat wok, add oil and swirl to heat. Stir-fry crab halves for 5 minutes and remove to a dish.
3 Reduce heat and stir-fry garlic, chillies and ginger for 3 minutes, then add chilli paste, tomato sauce, sugar and soy sauce. Mix well and bring to the boil.
4 Return crabs to the wok, stir well and simmer for 5 minutes, adding a little water or stock if the dish is in danger of drying out. Serve immediately.

Minty Barbecue Fish Cakes

Of Indonesian origin, these fish cakes are usually served with rice. Vietnamese or Cambodian mint, used in this recipe, is also known as Laksa.

PREPARATION TIME: *15 minutes*
COOKING TIME: *10 minutes*
SERVES 6

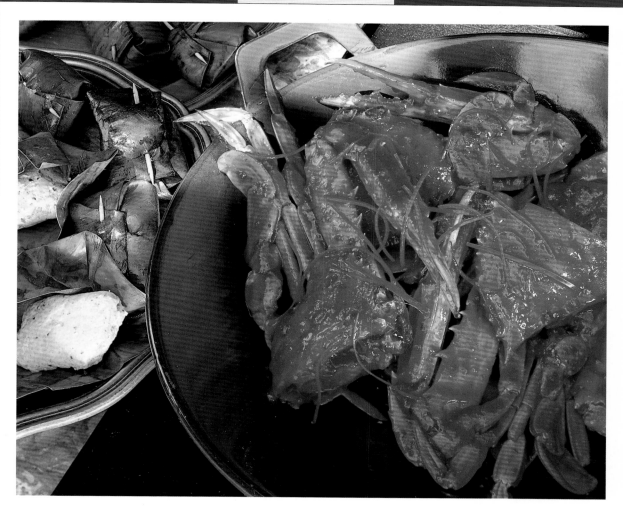

500 g firm white fish fillets
1 medium brown onion,
chopped
3 macadamia nuts or 6 cashew nuts
1 teaspoon chilli powder
½ teaspoon turmeric
1 tablespoon finely chopped fresh
lemon grass
1 teaspoon finely chopped
Vietnamese mint (optional)
½ teaspoon ground black pepper
salt, to taste
1 tablespoon sugar
½ cup thick coconut milk
1 tablespoon ground roasted dried
coriander
pieces of banana leaf
or baking paper, 16 cm square

1   Remove any small bones from the fish fillets. Cut into large pieces, about 3 cm square. Combine in a food processor with the remaining ingredients until smooth. Alternatively, finely chop the fish with a cleaver to make a paste and mix in the remaining ingredients.

2   Soften the banana leaves in boiling water for 1-2 minutes. Dry with absorbent paper. Place 2 tablespoons of the fish mixture onto a piece of banana leaf and fold into a packet. Fasten with a toothpick. Repeat with the remaining filling. If banana leaves are unavailable use squares of baking paper, then wrap the paper in foil the same size.

3   Place fish parcels on a preheated barbecue flat plate. Cook for 5 minutes each side or until fish is cooked.

Note: Vietnamese mint may also be added to main course dishes or soups.

Left: Minty Barbecue Fish Cakes. Right: Chilli Crab

Seafood Sauce
Combine 1 cup mayonnaise with 2 tablespoons tomato sauce, 2 teaspoons Worcestershire sauce, Tabasco sauce, lemon juice and black pepper to taste in a small bowl. Serve with prawns, oysters and other cooked seafood.

Mexican Fish Cakes in Corn Husks

Cooking corn with the husks protects it from the intense heat of the barbecue. If cooking corn without the husks, wrap in foil or place on the coolest part of the barbecue, allowing extra time for cobs to cook through.

PREPARATION TIME: *30 minutes +*
10 minutes standing
COOKING TIME: *20 minutes*
SERVES 4

4 corn cobs, complete with husks
450 g firm white fish fillets, diced
2 cloves garlic, crushed
2 teaspoons Mexican chilli powder (see Note)
⅓ cup finely chopped fresh coriander
1 tablespoon chopped canned jalapeno chillies
1 egg beaten
½ teaspoon ground black pepper
1 tablespoon lemon juice
2 tablespoons chopped spring onions
1 teaspoon ground cumin
foil squares, for wrapping

1 Remove only four husks from each corn cob and set aside. Turn back the remaining husks (being careful not to detach them) and remove the thread-like cornsilk. Pull the husks back into position to enclose the corn. Soak the cobs in cold water for 10-15 minutes.
2 Process fish in a processor until just smooth, combine with remaining ingredients. Divide into eight equal portions.
3 Wrap each portion in two of the reserved corn husks taken from the corn cobs. Then wrap parcels in squares of foil.
4 Start grilling the corn on barbecue for 20 minutes, turning them once or twice.
5 Place wrapped fish cakes on medium hot flat plate during last 8 minutes and both should be ready at the same time.
Note: Mexican chilli powder is available in all supermarket spice ranges. It contains a mixture of paprika, chillies, cumin and oregano.

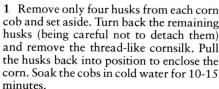

Tartare Sauce
Add ¼ cup chopped gherkins, 1 tablespoon chopped capers, 2 tablespoons chopped red capsicum and 2 tablespoons chopped parsley to 1½ cups mayonnaise, mix well. Serve with hot or cold seafoods.

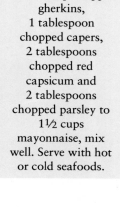

Set aside 4 husks. Remove cornsilk. Pull remaining husks back into position.

Process fish and remaining ingredients in food processor until just smooth.

Wrap each portion of fish in two of the corn husks taken from the corn cobs.

Wrap each corn parcel in squares of aluminium foil and cook for 8 minutes.

Mexican Fish Cakes in Corn Husks

No matter the type of seafood you're after, one rule always applies: buy from a reputable fishmonger. If it's busy all the time, it's a good indication that the stock is turning over regularly. Stay away from the store which has strong fishy odours as opposed to a fresh, seaside fragrance. When purchasing whole fish, look for bright and bulging eyes. The flesh should be firm and gills bright pink. Ask the fish shop to gut and scale the fish that you have selected.

Seafood Kebabs

Serve these delicious Seafood Kebabs with a variety of salads and crusty bread.

PREPARATION TIME: *15 minutes +*
15 minutes marinating
COOKING TIME: *7 minutes*
SERVES *6-8*

750 g firm white fish fillets
18 large green prawns
18 scallops
1 red capsicum
1 green capsicum
1 yellow capsicum

MARINADE
3 tablespoons olive oil
3 tablespoons lemon juice
2 teaspoons chopped fresh dill
½ teaspoon salt
½ teaspoon white pepper

lemon wedges, to serve

1 Remove skin from the fillets if necessary. Cut into 3 cm square pieces. Peel and devein the prawns. Cut the red, green and yellow capsicum into pieces the same size as the fish. Place prepared ingredients in a bowl.
2 To make Marinade: Combine all the ingredients. Pour over the fish and turn to coat. Allow to marinate for 15 minutes.
3 Thread the ingredients alternately onto soaked bamboo skewers or metal skewers.
4 Cook kebabs on a preheated oiled flat plate until fish turns white and prawns are pink and opaque. Serve immediately with lemon wedges and a tartare sauce.
Note: Soaking the bamboo skewers is a must when barbecuing. The longer they soak, the less they'll burn. Wrap foil around the exposed end to prevent scorching. If using metal skewers it may be necessary to reduce the cooking time slightly. To make a quick Tartare Sauce: Add ¼ cup chopped gherkins, 1 tablespoon chopped capers, 2 tablespoons chopped red capsicum and 2 tablespoons chopped parsley to 1½ cups mayonnaise, mix well. Serve with hot or cold seafoods.

Tandoori Prawns

Although this recipe is not cooked in a tandoor oven, you will be more than happy with the result.

PREPARATION TIME: *20 minutes +*
15 minutes marinating
COOKING TIME: *5 minutes*
SERVES *6 as entrée,*
3-4 as main meal

24 large green prawns
½ cup plain yoghurt
⅓ cup finely chopped fresh
coriander leaves
2 tablespoons finely chopped mint leaves
salt, to taste
1 tablespoon chopped fresh ginger
2 cloves garlic, crushed
1 teaspoon chilli powder
1 teaspoon turmeric
1 teaspoon ground coriander
1 teaspoon garam masala
few drops bright red food colouring
(optional)

2 lemons, cut into wedges, to serve

1 Shell and de-vein the prawns, leaving only the tail on. Rinse and pat dry.
2 Combine yoghurt with fresh coriander, mint and salt to taste. Pour over the prawns and leave for 5 minutes.
3 Mix together the remaining ingredients and use to marinate the prawns for 10 minutes.
4 Thread the prawns onto metal skewers and cook on elevated charcoal grill for about 5 minutes. Turn the skewers so the prawns cook evenly. Prawns are ready when they start to curl and turn opaque. Serve with lemon wedges.
Note: Complement this dish with a tomato onion sambal. Finely chop one medium tomato that has been peeled and seeded, combine with one small finely chopped white or purple onion. Add some lime or lemon juice to moisten. Or try the following cool Cucumber and Yoghurt Sauce: Peel a large cucumber, cut in half and scoop out the seeds. Finely chop cucumber flesh, sprinkle with a little salt and stand for 5-6 minutes. Drain off the accumulated liquid. Add cucumber to ½ cup plain yoghurt and two teaspoons chopped mint.

Above: Seafood Kebabs. Below: Tandoori Prawns

Easy Vegetables, Salads, Breads & Sauces

SELECT FROM A variety of vegetables and crisp salad greens for a complete barbecue meal or an accompaniment. Serve salads with a selection of dressings containing flavoured vinegars and oils, combined with mustards and seasonings.

Breads are also an essential accompaniment to any barbecue. Garlic and herb breads are easy to prepare and can be cooked directly on the barbecue. If time is short, choose a variety of rolls, loaves and sticks and serve with mildly flavoured butters.

Make a selection from the dishes to follow for a smorgasbord of vegetarian delights. They are there to make your vegetarian barbecuing a little more exciting. During autumn when salads are scarce, vegetables and tasty vegetarian main dishes can be a welcome addition to the menu for barbecue parties and entertaining for all occasions.

Above: Golden Nugget Vegetable Slice (page 80). Left: Vegetable Kebabs (page 80). Right: Damper (page 95)

Pumpkin Parcels
Wash a small butternut pumpkin and cut into 2 cm slices. Place each slice on a folded piece of foil, four layers thick and about 10 cm square. (This will ensure the pumpkin does not burn on the bottom with its natural sweetness.)
Top with a little butter, sprinkle with nutmeg, ½ teaspoon honey and white pepper. Enclose the pumpkin slices and folded foil in another sheet of foil, making a seam on the top.
Place on a heated barbecue grill. Cook for 30-35 minutes or until the pumpkin is tender.

Vegetable Kebabs

For extra flavour, serve with one of the flavoured butters see page 21.

PREPARATION TIME: *20 minutes*
COOKING TIME: *15 minutes*
SERVES 6

6 small onions
12 button mushrooms
2 small zucchini
1 red capsicum
12 large cherry tomatoes

MARINADE
½ cup olive oil
2 tablespoons lemon juice
1 teaspoon lemon pepper
2 teaspoons chopped fresh thyme
or ½ teaspoon dried thyme

1 Peel the onions and blanch in boiling water for 5 minutes or until barely tender. Drain, cool in iced water and set aside.
2 Trim the mushrooms, slice the zucchini and cut the capsicum into large pieces. Thread all the vegetables and tomatoes alternately onto skewers and place in a shallow dish.
3 To make Marinade: Combine all the ingredients and pour over the vegetables. Allow to marinate for 30 minutes, turning occasionally.
4 Cook kebabs on preheated barbecue for 8 minutes or until vegetables are tender, turning after 4 minutes and basting from time to time with the remaining marinade.
Note: When buying cherry tomatoes for kebabs, choose them hard and firm so they will stay on the skewers when barbecued. Use any fresh seasonal vegetables for this recipe. When purchasing vegetables, always select items free from blemishes and decay. Vegetables that have been grown locally and purchased in season are less costly than those imported when they otherwise would not be available.

Golden Nugget Vegetable Slice

Prepare these stuffed pumpkins up to the final stages of cooking, set aside and finish the cooking just prior to serving.

PREPARATION TIME: *10 minutes*
COOKING TIME: *10 minutes*
SERVES 6-8

2 golden nugget pumpkins

FILLING
4 spring onions, chopped
10 green beans, chopped
½ red capsicum, chopped
1 small seedless cucumber,
  halved and chopped
1 clove garlic, crushed
3 teaspoons beef stock powder
1 teaspoon turmeric
½ teaspoon ground pepper
½ cup pecan pieces
½ cup fresh breadcrumbs
2 teaspoons Worcestershire sauce
3 tablespoons olive oil

1 Remove the tops from the nugget pumpkins and remove the seeds with a spoon and discard. Cover with plastic wrap and microwave on High (100%) for 3 minutes. Allow to stand while you prepare the filling. Or blanch pumpkin in boiling water until barely tender, drain and cool under running water.
2 Blend spring onions, beans, capsicum and cucumber until finely chopped in a food processor. Add remaining ingredients and mix well. Spoon the mixture into the nugget pumpkins.
3 Barbecue over high heat for 10 minutes.
4 Cut each pumpkin into three slices or into quarters to serve.
Note: If preferred, substitute the pumpkins for twelve medium mushrooms caps. Cook directly on the barbecue for 4-5 minutes. Serve immediately. Pumpkins can also be cooked in a moderate oven 180°C for about 15-20 minutes or until tender. Larger zucchini may also be used for this recipe. Slice in half lengthwise and remove the centre with a small teaspoon. Place the stuffing inside hollow, barbecue over low heat 8 minutes.

Quick and Easy Barbecued Vegetables

When friends drop in at the last minute and you decide to have a barbecue, these simple and delicious vegetables will surely impress. Frozen corn cobs can be used in place of fresh corn. Defrost before cooking on the barbecue.

PREPARATION TIME: *5 minutes*
COOKING TIME: *18 minutes*
SERVES 4 *as an accompaniment*

4 corn cobs
4 medium-large zucchini
2 tablespoons olive oil

SEASONING MIX
2 teaspoons lemon pepper seasoning
1 teaspoon onion powder

1 Remove the husks from the corn and rinse in cold water. Trim zucchini and cut in half lengthways. Blanch the corn cobs in boiling water for 6 minutes and the zucchini for about 3 minutes. Drop into iced water to cool, drain and pat dry with absorbent paper.
2 Brush the prepared vegetables with olive oil and sprinkle with combined seasonings. Place in a baking tray.
3 Place tray on the barbecue and cook about 8 minutes. with the hood down, turning occasionally or until vegetables are heated through and tender. Serve immediately. If using a barbecue without a hood, cook vegetables covered with heavy-duty or industrial-strength foil. Serve with flavoured butter (see page 21).
Note: Seasoned pepper is available in most supermarkets. It is a combination of peppercorns, red bell pepper, garlic and paprika. Or combine 3 tablespoons ground pepper with 2 teaspoons garlic powder and 1 tablespoon ground sweet paprika. Store in an airtight jar.

Brighten up your kebabs with coloured squash. When choosing baby squash, select both yellow and green for appearance.

Quick and Easy Barbecued Vegetables

For a change, serve a hot potato salad for your next barbecue. Boil baby new potatoes in their jackets, halve and add chopped gherkins and enough mayonnaise to combine. Season with pepper and serve warm.

Spicy Mint Potatoes

Spicy Mint Potatoes

This subtle combination of sharp cheese and spicy curry powder helps lift the humble potato to new heights of flavour.

PREPARATION TIME: *25 minutes*
COOKING TIME: *30 minutes*
SERVES 6

6 medium potatoes
30 g butter
¼ cup lemon juice
3 teaspoon chicken stock powder
2 tablespoons hot milk
½ cup finely chopped fresh mint
2 spring onions, finely chopped
½ cup grated Cheddar cheese
1 teaspoon mild curry powder

1 Wash potatoes and prick with a fork or skewer. Place evenly around the turntable of the microwave. Cook washed potates on High (100%) for 12 minutes, allow to stand for 10 minutes. Or cook potatoes on a rack in a moderate oven 180°C for about 30 minutes or until just tender. Cut the potatoes in half and scoop out the centres. Place the shells on a deep baking tray and the potato flesh into a bowl.
2 Mash the potato flesh and add the butter, lemon juice, chicken stock powder and milk. Mix until smooth. Add chopped mint and spring onion. Spoon the mixture into the potato shells.
3 Combine cheese with curry powder and sprinkle on top of the potato. Cover the tray with foil.
4 Place tray on preheated barbecue and cook over moderate heat for about 15 minutes or until potatoes are hot and cheese is bubbly.

Garlic Buttered Corn Cobs

Serve these deliciously flavoured corn cobs as an accompaniment to meat. Use cob-holders for inserting in the ends – this makes them a little easier to eat.

PREPARATION TIME: *15 minutes*
COOKING TIME: *18 minutes*
SERVES 6 *as an accompaniment*

6 corn cobs
90 g butter, softened
1 clove garlic, crushed
¼ teaspoon ground pepper
½ cup grated Cheddar cheese

1 Remove husks and silks from the corn cobs and trim away any excess stalk. Place the cobs in a pan of boiling water and simmer for 8 minutes.
2 Combine softened butter, crushed garlic, pepper and cheese. Brush mixture over the corn cobs.
3 Wrap each cob of corn in a double layer of heavy-duty or industrial-strength foil.
4 Preheat the barbecue and place the wrapped corn cobs onto the flat plate or grill. Barbecue for 10 minutes, turning once during cooking. Remove foil and serve immediately.

Above: Garlic Buttered Corn Cobs. Below: Chilli Mushroom Caps (page 85)

Marinated Barbecued Mushrooms

For best results use white button mushrooms, fully closed; the firmer, the better.

PREPARATION TIME: *10 minutes*
COOKING TIME: *2-5 minutes*
SERVES 4-6

500 g firm button mushrooms
¼ cup olive oil
1 clove garlic, crushed
2 tablespoons lime juice
salt and pepper, to taste

1 Wipe any dirt from mushrooms with damp absorbent paper. Trim ends off stems and discard. Slice mushrooms, not too thinly.
2 In a bowl, combine oil, garlic, lime juice, salt and pepper. Toss sliced mushrooms in this dressing and allow to stand about half an hour before cooking.
3 Cook mushrooms over a high heat on the barbecue flat plate. Toss mushroom slices constantly until starting to brown. Serve as a side dish to meat or chicken.

Sliced Stuffed Potatoes
Slice medium potatoes at 1 cm intervals, keeping them attached at the bottom. Fill the slits with finely sliced spring onions. Sprinkle with pepper and garlic powder, dot with butter. Wrap each potato in foil and cook on a hot grill for about 40 minutes or until tender. Serve immediately.

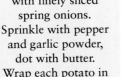

Left: Marinated Barbecued Mushrooms. Right: Stuffed Pumpkins with Cheesy Sauce

Stuffed Pumpkins with Cheesy Sauce

These stuffed pumpkins are a meal in one. Make them in advance and set aside. Do the final stages of cooking when ready to serve. Two medium butternut pumpkins can be used.

PREPARATION TIME: *35 minutes*
COOKING TIME: *35 minutes*
SERVES 8

8 golden nugget pumpkins
3 small carrots, peeled
3 small zucchini
100 g mushrooms
1 large potato, peeled
100 g green beans
3 tablespoons olive oil
2 onions, finely chopped
1 clove garlic, crushed

SAUCE
30 g butter
¼ cup plain flour
¾ cup cream
¾ cup milk
1 cup grated Cheddar cheese
2 tablespoons chopped chives
salt and pepper, to taste

1 Remove the tops from the pumpkins and scoop out the seeds with a spoon. Place the pumpkins and tops in a large baking tray, with 3 tablespoons water, cover with foil and bake in a hot oven 200°C for 20 minutes or until tender. Allow to cool.
2 Slice carrots, zucchini and mushrooms and dice the potato. Top and tail the beans and cut into bite-size pieces.
3 Heat the olive oil in a large pan and cook the onion and garlic until soft and golden. Add the carrots and potatoes. Stir to coat with the butter, cover and cook the vegetables over a low heat for 5 minutes. Add the remaining vegetables and cook covered, until vegetables are tender, adding a little water from time to time to prevent them catching.
4 To make Sauce: In a seperate pan, melt butter and add flour. Stir over a moderate heat for 1-2 minutes. Remove the pan from the heat and add the cream and milk. Continue to cook, stirring until sauce sim-

mers and thickens. Add half grated cheese, chives, salt and pepper to taste.

5 Add the sauce to the vegetables and mix well. Spoon the prepared vegetables into the pumpkin cases. Sprinkle with a little extra cheese and replace the tops. Place into a baking tray, with a little water to prevent them burning. Cover with foil and set aside.

6 Place onto a preheated barbecue grill and cook for 10-15 minutes or until cheese melts and pumpkins are heated through. Serve immediately.

Chilli Mushroom Caps

The important thing about this recipe is not to turn the mushrooms during the cooking. As the butter melts down the stalk of the mushroom, the cap catches the butter along with all the mushroom juices.

PREPARATION TIME: *10 minutes*
COOKING TIME: *5-7 minutes*
SERVES *6*

12 large mushrooms

CHILLI BUTTER
60 g butter, softened
2 teaspoons hot chilli sauce
1 teaspoon crushed garlic
1 teaspoon ground sweet paprika
½ teaspoon garam masala

1 Wipe the mushroom caps with damp absorbent paper and slice off the stalks almost level with the outer edge. Set aside on a tray so they can be easily transported to the barbecue.

2 To make Chilli Butter: Combine the softened butter with remaining ingredients and mix until thoroughly combined. Place a portion of butter on the top of each mushroom stalk.

3 Arrange the mushrooms cap side down on a hot barbecue flat plate. Cook for 5-7 minutes or until the butter melts and serve immediately. The Chilli Mushroom Caps are delicious as a side dish with steaks and as a starter with bread.

Note: Garam masala is a mixture of ground spices including peppercorns, cardamom and cloves.

Ratatouille

A flavoursome combination of vegetables. Make in advance and warm in a large pan on the edge of the barbecue. Makes an ideal accompaniment to poultry. This can also be a perfect vegetarian meal for four people when served with crusty bread rolls.

PREPARATION TIME: *25 minutes*
COOKING TIME: *40 minutes*
SERVES *8 as an accompaniment*

2 large eggplant
4 medium zucchini
2 red capsicum
2 green capsicum
1 x 425 g can peeled tomatoes
2 large potatoes
⅓ cup olive oil
2 large onions, chopped
2 large cloves garlic, crushed
1 teaspoon dried basil
¼ cup chopped fresh coriander
2 teaspoons garlic pepper seasoning

1 Wash the eggplant, zucchini and capsicum. Cut eggplant into large pieces and thickly slice zucchini. Remove seeds from the capsicum and cut into large pieces. Drain tomatoes, reserving the liquid and roughly chop. Peel potatoes and cut into large dice.

2 Heat olive oil in a large pan or wok and cook onions and garlic until onions are tender. Add the prepared eggplant, zucchini and capsicum. Cook for 1-2 minutes. Add the tomatoes and reserved juice with the potatoes, basil, coriander and garlic pepper seasoning. Cover and cook, adding a little water to prevent sticking if necessary, for 30 minutes or until the vegetables are tender.

3 Serve hot immediately or warm on the edge of the barbecue, stirring occasionally until heated.

Note: If you enjoy a more fiery dish, try adding 2 teaspoons of sambal olek with the peeled tomatoes. Sambal olek is a prepared chilli relish of Indonesian origin, containing chilli, garlic and salt. It is used as a flavour enhancer, making the dish hotter and more appetising. Sambal olek is available from most supermarkets and Asian food stores.

Crispy-topped Tomatoes
Melt 40 g butter in a small pan, add 1 clove garlic, crushed, 1 tablespoon chopped fresh herbs and 1 cup fresh breadcrumbs. Cook until the crumbs brown lightly. Halve four tomatoes, sprinkle with pepper and top with crispy crumbs. Place in a tray and cook on preheated barbecue for 8 – 10 minutes or until heated through.

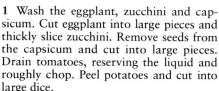

Hot Mushrooms and Tomato

When making foil parcels for the barbecue, use a double thickness of foil.

PREPARATION TIME: *10 minutes*
COOKING TIME: *10 minutes*
SERVES 6

375 g button mushrooms
3 tomatoes, finely diced
6 spring onions, finely chopped
2 teaspoons herb pepper seasoning
60 g butter
Tabasco sauce, to taste

1 Wipe the mushrooms and place evenly into the base of six small foil pie plates. Alternatively prepare six squares of heavy-duty or industrial-strength foil.
2 Put diced tomatoes and chopped spring onions into pie plates or on foil squares. Sprinkle each parcel with herb pepper-seasonings to taste. Dot the tops of each parcel with a little butter and Tabasco sauce. Cover foil plates with foil or enclose ingredients in the prepared foil squares.
3 Place on the outer edge of a preheated barbecue grill and cook for 10 minutes or until heated through. Serve immediately as a side dish to meat and poultry.

Whether to chop, finely chop, dice or cube can often be confusing. So follow this guide. To cube, the pieces should be about 2 cm square. To dice, the pieces are about 1 cm. To finely chop, the food should be cut small, no more than about 3 mm square.

Hot Mushrooms and Tomato

Broccoli and Cauliflower with Sesame Soy Dressing

If your barbecue set-up does not include a wok, it can easily be prepared back in the kitchen. Simply steam the broccoli and cauliflower over a little boiling water or microwave until tender. Prepare the sauce in a small pan and spoon over the vegetables when ready to serve.

PREPARATION TIME: *10 minutes*
COOKING TIME: *4 minutes*
SERVES 6

4 cups water
4 cups broccoli florets
4 cups cauliflower florets

SAUCE
3 tablespoons dry sherry
2 tablespoons water
3 tablespoons dark soy sauce
(see Note)
2 teaspoons grated
fresh green ginger
2 teaspoons sugar
½ cup toasted sesame seeds,
crushed
2 teaspoons cornflour
3 tablespoons water

1 Bring water to the boil in a wok or large pan. Drop in broccoli and cauliflower, boil covered for 4 minutes. Drain and place on serving dish.
2 To make Sauce: Place sherry, water, soy sauce, ginger, sugar and crushed sesame seeds in the wok. Bring to a boil. Meanwhile, combine cornflour and water, and add to the simmering mixture. Stir until thickened and pour over broccoli and cauliflower. Serve with barbecued fish.
Note: Dark soy sauce is less salty and more caramelised than the lighter styles of soy sauces available.
Use the stems from the broccoli and cauliflower in stir-fry dishes. Just thinly peel away any tough outer skins. The inner stem is usually tender.
Toast sesame seeds over a moderate heat in a dry pan, stirring continuously until they begin to turn golden. Serve immediately.

Above: Ratatouille (page 85). Below: Broccoli and Cauliflower with Sesame Soy Dressing

Avocado, Mango and Walnut Salad

This exquisite salad will prove to be a great success at your barbecues.

PREPARATION TIME: *15 minutes*
COOKING TIME: *5 minutes*
SERVES 6

3 bacon rashers
1 mignonette lettuce
2 mangoes
2 avocados
½ cup walnut halves

DRESSING
¼ cup olive oil
2 tablespoons lemon juice
1 teaspoon French mustard
1 tablespoon thickened cream

1 Remove the rind from the bacon and roughly chop. Cook bacon in a lightly oiled pan until crisp. Allow to cool on absorbent paper.
2 Wash lettuce, separate the leaves, dry gently and place in a serving bowl.
3 A short time before required, peel and slice mangoes and avocados. Arrange over the lettuce and sprinkle with chopped bacon and walnut halves. Cover with plastic wrap but do not chill as the flavours are best at room temperature.
4 To make Dressing: Place ingredients in a small bowl and whisk until well combined. Drizzle over the Avocado, Mango and Walnut Salad when ready to serve.
Note: As a special touch add 1 tablespoon of walnut oil to the dressing.

Tomato and Mozzarella Salad

The addition of capers gives a special, piquant touch to this easy salad.

PREPARATION TIME: *10 minutes*
COOKING TIME: *Nil*
SERVES 8

Fruit Vinegar Dressing
Combine in a screw-top jar with a tight-fitting lid, 4 tablespoons fruit or herb vinegar, 2 tablespoons chopped fresh herbs, ½ teaspoon dry mustard, 1 cup salad oil or olive oil, pinch sugar and salt and ground pepper to taste. Shake well. Use in salads or drizzle over avocado.

Use a selection of bean sprouts, alfalfa, snow pea sprouts and watercress in salads to add variety.

6 firm, ripe tomatoes
250 g mozzarella cheese, thinly sliced
1 small purple onion, finely chopped
20 fresh basil leaves, finely chopped
1 tablespoon capers

DRESSING
3 tablespoons extra virgin olive oil
1 tablespoon lemon juice
salt and pepper, to taste

1 Slice tomato 3 mm thick and alternate with slices of cheese in a large serving dish. Sprinkle with chopped onion, basil and capers.
2 To make Dressing: Combine all the ingredients in a small bowl. Drizzle over salad when ready to serve.
Note: Extra virgin olive oil gives a unique flavour, but a good quality olive oil may be used in its place.

Five Bean Salad

Mung bean sprouts add that extra crunch to this bean salad. Serve with barbecued meats or as a hearty accompaniment to a vegetarian meal.

PREPARATION TIME: *10 minutes*
COOKING TIME: *Nil*
SERVES 8-10

⅓ cup mayonnaise
1 small purple onion
or 2 spring onions, chopped
ground pepper, to taste
1 x 250 g tub mung bean sprouts
1 x 750 g can four-bean mix, drained
1 x 440 g can corn kernels, drained
¼ cup currants
2 tablespoons sultanas
1 red capsicum, diced
¼ cup pecan pieces, toasted

1 In a large bowl mix together mayonnaise, onion and pepper. Add all the other ingredients, except pecans, and mix well. Cover with plastic wrap. Chill.
2 Toss salad just before serving. Sprinkle top with pecans to garnish.
Note: Purple or Spanish onions are milder than their pungent brown or white cousins, and ideal in salads.

Clockwise from top: Avocado, Mango and Walnut Sauce, Tomato and Mozzarella Salad, Five Bean Salad

Rice Salad with Lime

This quick and easy rice salad is an ideal way to give cooked rice a bit of a lift.

PREPARATION TIME: *10 minutes*
COOKING TIME: *Nil*
SERVES 6

4 cups cold cooked rice
2 seedless cucumbers, diced
1 red capsicum, finely diced
1 cup finely chopped fresh coriander

DRESSING
3 tablespoons olive oil
2 tablespoons lime juice
2 teaspoons grated lime rind
1 teaspoon ground sweet paprika
½ teaspoon salt
1 clove garlic, crushed

1 Place rice in a bowl, add cucumbers, capsicum and coriander. Mix well.
2 To make Dressing: Combine all the ingredients and pour over the rice mixture. Toss lightly together and serve the rice salad immediately.
Note: Lime juice adds a particular flavour to this salad. As a second choice, lemon juice can be used if limes are not available.

Rice Salad with Lime

Potato Salad

If you're using a store-bought mayonnaise, be sure to choose a sharp tasting one for the best result.

PREPARATION TIME: *20 minutes*
COOKING TIME: *10 minutes*
SERVES *8-10*

8 medium potatoes, scrubbed well
or peeled
1 medium orange sweet potato
1 medium white sweet potato
½ cup mayonnaise
¾ cup sour cream
ground pepper, to taste
1 purple onion, finely chopped
1 red capsicum, diced
1 yellow or green capsicum, diced
250 g leg ham, cut into slivers

1 Peel and cut potatoes and sweet potato into small cubes. Cook in boiling water for 5 minutes, or until tender but not mushy. Drain.
2 In a large bowl, mix mayonnaise, sour cream, seasonings and onions together. Add cooked, drained potatoes while hot. Gently stir in capsicum and ham until just combined. Serve while warm or cover, refrigerate overnight and serve chilled.
Note: It is important to cut the potatoes into equal sizes for even cooking. This method of preparing the potatoes shortens cooking time and ensures that the potatoes are not starchy in the middle, which sometimes happens when they are cooked whole.

Apple and Pear Waldorf

When available use nashi fruit. They are easy to purchase at most green-grocers. If nashi are out of season, use firm, crisp pears as an alternative.

PREPARATION TIME: *20 minutes*
COOKING TIME: *Nil*
SERVES *8-10*

2 crisp red apples
2 pears or nashi fruit
¼ cup lemon juice
1 stick celery, sliced
½ cup walnut
or pecan pieces
½ cup mayonnaise
1 tablespoon shredded pickled
ginger (optional)
½ teaspoon white pepper
1 tablespoon toasted sesame seeds
(optional)

1 Core and dice apples and pears. Toss in lemon juice to prevent fruit from discolouring.
2 Reserving a teaspoon each of sesame seeds and ginger for the garnish, combine remaining ingredients, mixing well. Add fruit, stirring to coat the apples and pears with dressing. Sprinkle over reserved sesame seeds and scatter with ginger.
Note: Shredded pickled ginger has a distinctive pink colour and sweet-salty flavour. It is available in Asian food stores.

Above: Apple and Pear Waldorf. Below Potato Salad

Capsicum and Spring Onion Salad

A Middle Eastern vegetarian salad which can also feature as a main course.

PREPARATION TIME: *20 minutes*
COOKING TIME: *8 minutes*
SERVES 8 *as a salad*, 4 *as a meal*

4 wholemeal or plain pitta bread rounds
½ cup grapefruit or lemon juice
¼ cup olive oil
2 tablespoons water
3 teaspoons chilli sauce
salt and pepper, to taste
2 cloves garlic, crushed
1 cup chopped spring onions, white and green sections
1 cup chopped fresh coriander leaves
½ cup chopped fresh flat-leaved parsley
¼ cup chopped fresh mint
2 seeded tomatoes, chopped
2 medium red capsicum, diced
1 medium green capsicum, diced
1 stalk celery, chopped
2 Lebanese cucumbers, diced

1 Gently pull apart the two layers of each pitta so that you have two very thin rounds. Place in a preheated oven 200°C for 8 minutes or until golden brown in colour. Remove and set aside to cool.

2 In a large salad bowl or mixing bowl, combine the grapefruit juice, olive oil, water, chilli sauce, salt, pepper and crushed garlic and swirl bowl to coat sides.
3 Add all other ingredients (except bread) to bowl and mix well.
4 Break bread into medium-small pieces, add to the bowl and toss thoroughly. Serve immediately in order to retain the crispness which is a feature of this salad.

Red Cabbage Salad

Raw beetroot is packed with nutrition but its earthy, sweet taste does not necessarily appeal to everyone. Substitute with the same amount of grated red or green apple if you prefer.

PREPARATION TIME: *20 minutes*
COOKING TIME: *Nil*
SERVES 8-10

½ red cabbage, shredded
3 medium carrots, grated
1 medium raw beetroot, peeled and grated
1 red capsicum, seeded and finely sliced
3 spring onions, chopped
1 orange, peeled and diced
1 x 440 g unsweetened pineapple pieces in natural juice

DRESSING
1 egg, room temperature
1 teaspoon dry mustard
salt and pepper, to taste
1 tablespoon honey
1 tablespoon cider vinegar
1 tablespoon raspberry or white wine vinegar
¼ cup vegetable oil

1 In a large bowl, combine cabbage, carrots, beetroot, capsicum, spring onions and orange. Drain the pineapple pieces and add to the salad. Toss well.
2 To make Dressing: Place egg, dry mustard, salt and pepper, honey and vinegars into blender, process until smooth.
3 With the motor still running, gradually add the oil to the egg mixture. Blend until the oil is incorporated and the mixture is thick and creamy. Pour dressing over salad, toss through and serve.

Always purchase good quality salad ingredients and store them in the refrigerator as soon as possible. Wash items well and allow to dry, store in large airtight containers if you have them. Alternatively, you can prolong the life of your salad greens by placing in plastic bags, securely closed.

Capsicum and Spring Onion Salad

Above: Savoury Cornbread (page 94). Below: Red Cabbage Salad

Garlic or Herbed Bread Rolls

Choose long French sticks or small baton-type bread rolls for this quick and easy, popular recipe.

PREPARATION TIME: *15 minutes*
COOKING TIME: *8 minutes*
SERVES *8*

GARLIC BUTTER
125 g butter, softened
¼ cup olive oil
3 cloves garlic, crushed
1 tablespoon finely chopped parsley
¼ teaspoon ground pepper

HERB BUTTER
125 g butter, softened
¼ cup olive oil
2 tablespoons finely chopped
spring onions
4 tablespoons chopped fresh parsley
2 tablespoons chopped fresh chives
or 2 teaspoons dried mixed herbs
¼ teaspoon white pepper

2 long French loaves or
8 small baton loaves

1 Prepare flavoured butter of your choice. Combine softened butter with the remaining ingredients. Cut French loaf or rolls into thick slices and spread with prepared butter. Reassemble the loaf and wrap it tightly in heavy-duty or industrial-strength foil, with the join at the top.

2 Place on a preheated barbecue and cook for 8 minutes turning often or until heated through. Serve immediately.
Note: Make this recipe ahead and refrigerate. Before the guests arrive allow it to come to room temperature and pop it on the barbecue to cook. Or cook in a moderate oven 180°C for 15 minutes.

Savoury Cornbread

Whether hot off the barbecue or straight from the oven, the aroma alone of this superb bread will tempt even the fussiest guest. Best cooked on a kettle barbecue.

PREPARATION TIME: *15 minutes*
COOKING TIME: *35 minutes*
SERVES *8*

60 g butter
2 tablespoons olive oil
½ cup finely chopped spring onions
1 clove garlic, crushed
2 canned jalapeno chillies, chopped
½ cup chopped coriander (see Note)
1 cup milk
1 egg, lightly beaten
1 cup self-raising flour
1 teaspoon salt
2 teaspoons baking powder
1 cup yellow cornmeal (polenta)
½ cup grated Cheddar cheese
¼ teaspoon ground sweet paprika

1 Melt butter, add olive oil, spring onions, garlic, chillies, chopped coriander, milk and egg. Mix well.
2 Sift the self-raising flour, salt, baking powder and cornmeal into a bowl. Add mixed ingredients. Beat to a smooth batter.
3 Pour the mixture into a lightly greased and lined 23 cm square baking dish. Sprinkle with grated cheese and paprika. Bake in a preheated moderately hot oven 190°C for 30 minutes or until cornbread is golden brown.
4 To barbecue: Preheat kettle barbecue to medium-high, then lower the heat. Place cornbread on a 5 cm rack which has been covered with a double layer of foil. Cook using indirect heat, hood down for 35 minutes or until the cornbread pulls away from the sides of the pan. Cut the Savoury Cornbread into squares, to serve.

Chilli Garlic Toast
Combine 125 g softened butter with 3 tablespoons olive oil, 3 teaspoons chilli powder, 1 teaspoon crushed garlic, ½ teaspoon salt and ½ teaspoon ground pepper, in a small bowl. Spread over 2 cm thick slices of French bread. Toast both sides over direct coals on a barbecue grill until golden. Serve immediately.

Garlic or Herbed Bread Rolls

Note: Coriander is a pungent fresh herb, similiar in appearance to flat-leaved parsley but smaller. It is available at leading fruit and vegetable shops and Asian food stores.

Damper

If preferred, sprinkle the top of this damper with ½ cup grated Cheddar cheese and a little ground sweet paprika. Best cooked on a kettle barbecue.

PREPARATION TIME: *15 minutes*
COOKING TIME: *30-35 minutes*
SERVES *8*

3 cups self-raising flour
1 teaspoon salt
80 g butter
250 mL milk
1 egg, lightly beaten
1 tablespoon sesame seeds
¼ teaspoon ground sweet paprika

1 Sift the flour and salt into a large bowl. Cut the butter into small portions and rub into the flour until the mixture resembles fine breadcrumbs.
2 Make a well in the centre and add the combined milk and beaten egg. Mix to a firm dough with a flat-bladed knife, bringing the mixture together with your hands. if necessary.
3 Form the dough into a round and place on a baking tray, lined with a double layer of heavy-duty foil, placed shiny side down. Pat out to 20 cm in diameter. Brush with a little water, sprinkle with sesame seeds and paprika.
4 Preheat kettle barbecue to medium-high. Cook damper on indirect heat, hood down for 25-35 minutes, elevated on a 5 cm rack. The damper should be firm and hollow sounding when tapped. Reduce heat to medium if damper browns too quickly. Alternatively, bake in a preheated moderate oven 180°C for 20 minutes or until loaf sounds hollow when tapped. Serve the damper immediately with butter.
Note: Damper can be made and shaped up to two hours in advance. Cover with plastic wrap and allow to stand at room temperature and cook in kettle barbecue or bake in oven when needed.

Cheese Bread

Be creative with this recipe. By using other combinations of cheese for variety. Best cooked on a kettle barbecue.

PREPARATION TIME: *15 minutes*
COOKING TIME: *8 minutes*
SERVES *8*

1 crusty French loaf
⅓ cup olive oil
125 g butter, softened
1 clove garlic, crushed
2 tablespoons French mustard
1 cup grated Cheddar cheese
1 cup grated mozzarella cheese
3 tablespoons sesame seeds

1 Slice the French loaf almost through, diagonally about 2 cm apart. Whip together olive oil, softened butter, crushed garlic and mustard until creamy.
2 Spread bread slices with whipped mixture and place on baking tray. Combine cheeses, sprinkle mixture between bread slices and top with sesame seeds.
3 Wrap bread in heavy-duty or industrial-strength foil. Place in a baking tray or cake tin on the flat plate of hot kettle barbecue. Cover and cook for 8 minutes or until cheese bubbles. Alternatively, bake the bread in a moderate oven 180°C for about 10 minutes.
Note: Be careful not to overcook. The bread will quickly become hard and the cheese leathery, spoiling the end result.

Grilled Cheese and Bread Skewers
For every two people cut a small baton loaf and 125 g mozzarella cheese into squares about the same size. Sprinkle cheese with salt and ground pepper. Alternate cubes of bread and cheese on metal skewers, beginning and ending with bread. Grill over medium heat, turning occasionally. Serve with olives and tossed green salad.

Cheese Bread

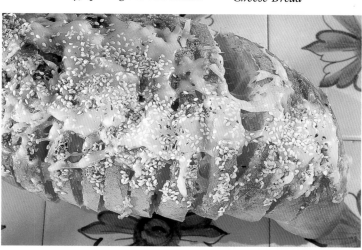

Simple Satay Sauce

Satay sauce can often be a chore to make. However, this recipe makes use of ready-to-use ingredients.

PREPARATION TIME: *10 minutes*
COOKING TIME: *5 minutes*
MAKES ABOUT *2½ cups*
USES: *With satays, lightly steamed vegetables, poultry and seafood*

1½ cups crunchy peanut butter
2 tablespoons soy sauce
1 tabelspoon sambal olek
2 teaspoons garlic powder
2 teaspoons onion powder
2 tablespoons brown sugar
1 teaspoon shrimp sauce (optional)
½ cup canned coconut milk
extra ½ cup water, for thinning

Heat peanut butter in a small pan together with the remaining ingredients, using the water to thin it down to a thick pouring consistency. Use as desired. Serve warm.
Note: Sambal olek is a paste made from crushed chillies. Available at most supermarkets and Asian food outlets.

Cashew Nut and Lime Juice Dressing
Combine the following ingredients in a blender or jar until smooth: ½ cup salted roasted cashews nuts, 1 teaspoon balsamic vinegar, 1½ tablespoons of lime juice, ½ cup water, ½ teaspoon crushed garlic, ½ teaspoon ground pepper and ½ teaspoon salt or to taste.

Barbecue Hollandaise Sauce

This is a great accompaniment to barbecued seafood and meats. It can turn the good old barbecued fish cutlets or prime beef steak into something your guests won't forget.

PREPARATION TIME: *20 minutes*
COOKING TIME: *5 minutes*
MAKES *1½ cups*
USES: *With seafood and meat dishes*

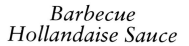

250 g butter
4 egg yolks, at room temperature
2 teaspoons lemon juice
2 teaspoons hot water
1 teaspoon Worcestershire sauce
cayenne pepper, to taste
2-3 tablespoons bottled barbecue sauce

1 Heat the butter until melted and allow to settle. Pour off the clear butter from the top, discarding the milky portion at the bottom.
2 Place egg yolks in a blender, add the lemon juice, hot water and Worcestershire sauce. Blend for 30 seconds or until light and creamy.
3 With the blender running, add the butter in a fine steady stream, blending until all the butter is added and sauce is thick. Transfer into a bowl.
4 Season to taste with pepper and barbecue sauce. Mix well. Serve at room temperature as an accompaniment.
Note: Ready-made barbecue sauce or hickory flavoured barbecue sauce can be used in this recipe.

Smoky Cajun Barbecue Sauce

If you have some of this Smoky Cajun Barbecue Sauce left over, store it in the refrigerator for use at a later date.

PREPARATION TIME: *10 minutes*
COOKING TIME: *15 minutes*
MAKES *1½ cups*
USES: *As a dipping sauce or accompaniment*

1 medium onion, grated
1 cup tomato sauce
⅓ cup sweet chilli sauce
1 tablespoon cider vinegar
⅓ cup brown sugar
5 cloves garlic, crushed
¾ teaspoon ground pepper
1 tablespoon liquid hickory smoke (optional)

1 Place all ingredients except liquid smoke, in an enamel-lined or flameproof glass pan.
2 Stir over low heat until sugar dissolves, then simmer for 12 minutes stirring occasionally. Remove from the heat, allow to cool and add the liquid smoke, if using.
3 Stir well and store in a glass jar in the refrigerator.
Note: If using liquid smoke, add one teaspoon at a time at the end of cooking, so you can adjust the quantity to suit your particular taste.

Tomato and Coriander Relish

Fresh relishes are full of flavour and so easy to make. Serve as an accompaniment.

PREPARATION TIME: *10 minutes*
MAKES ABOUT *3 cups*
USES: *Serve with satays, kebabs, vegetable dishes, breads and seafood*

3 firm ripe tomatoes, chopped
2 cups coriander leaves, chopped
juice of half a lime
1 teaspoon salt
1 teaspoon chilli powder (optional)
1 medium onion, finely chopped

Combine all ingredients and mix thoroughly. Serve as an accompaniment.
Note: This makes an appealing salad combination as well. Slice tomatoes and onions and arrange on a platter, sprinkle with the salt, chilli powder and coriander leaves. Combine lime juice with a little olive oil and drizzle over the salad to serve.

Sweet and Sour Sauce

This quick sweet and sour sauce is a great way to dress up barbecued fish. Try it as a dipping sauce for cooked king prawns and chicken nuggets.

PREPARATION TIME: *5 minutes*
COOKING TIME: *5 minutes*
MAKES *1 1/2 cups*
USES: *As a dipping sauce or accompaniment*

1/2 cup water
1/2 cup pineapple juice
1/4 cup white vinegar
1 tablespoon brown sugar
1/4 cup tomato sauce
1 tablespoon cornflour
1 tablespoon water

1 Place water, pineapple, vinegar, brown sugar and tomato sauce in a small pan.
2 Mix cornflour and water to a smooth paste. Add to the pan, stirring constantly over a medium heat until the sauce boils and thickens. Cool slightly before serving.

Creamy Coriander and Pepper Dressing
Combine 1/4 cup salad oil, 1/2 cup chopped coriander, 1/4 cup mayonnaise, 1/2 teaspoon crushed garlic, 2 tablespoons white wine vinegar, 1 tablespoon water, 1/2 teaspoon ground pepper and salt to taste in a blender. Blend until smooth and creamy. Use with tossed salad greens.

Clockwise from top left: Tomato and Coriander Relish, Simple Satay Sauce, Smoky Cajun Barbecue Sauce, Barbecue Hollandaise Sauce, Sweet and Sour Sauce

Sweet Barbecue Treats

HAVE LOADS OF sweet things to offer your guests. Strawberry Cheesecake, Baked Sweet Potato with Spiced Cream, Pineapple and Passionfruit Pavlova Roll, Bananas Jamaica, Oranges Le Hot – they're all here for you to choose from.

Some of these treats can be barbecued and some can be prepared ahead of time. Which ever way you choose to prepare them, the result will always be sensational.

Above: Vanilla Bananas (page 101). Below: Pineapple and Passionfruit Pavlova Roll (page 100)

Pineapple and Passionfruit Pavlova Roll

This pavlova roll recipe can be prepared well in advance and is a great conclusion to any barbecue.

Top your favourite pavlova recipe with sliced mango, pawpaw, kiwi fruit and some sweetened passionfruit pulp for a tropical touch to your barbecue.

PREPARATION TIME: *15 minutes*
COOKING TIME: *10 minutes*
SERVES 6

4 egg whites
⅔ cup caster sugar
1 tablespoon caster sugar, extra
¾ cup thickened cream
½ cup finely chopped canned pineapple pieces
3 tablespoons passionfruit pulp

TOPPING
extra whipped cream
pineapple pieces
passionfruit pulp
mint leaves (optional)

1 Place egg whites in a bowl and beat until soft peaks form. Add the caster sugar gradually, beating well after each addition. Spread the mixture into a lightly greased and paper lined 30 x 25 x 2 cm Swiss roll tin. Bake in a moderately hot oven 190°C for 10 minutes or until firm and golden.

Pineapple and Passionfruit Pavlova Roll

2 Sprinkle a sheet of baking paper with extra caster sugar and turn the pavlova onto the sheet, allow to cool completely.
3 Whip cream. Fold in finely chopped pineapple and passionfruit pulp. Spread cream over surface of the pavlova. Starting at the narrow end, roll the pavlova into a cylinder shape; use baking paper as a guide to help roll. Chill until serving.
4 Decorate with extra cream, pineapple, passionfruit and mint leaves if desired.
Note: When preparing the filling, make sure the pineapple pieces are well drained.

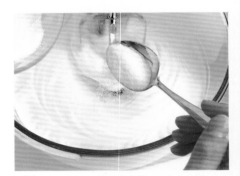

Add caster sugar gradually to beaten egg whites, beat well after each addition.

Sprinkle a sheet of baking paper with caster sugar and turn pavlova onto sheet.

Spread cream mixture over surface and roll pavlova into a cylinder shape.

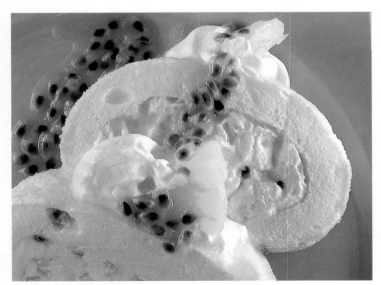

Hula Hula

The ground spices in this recipe are a taste sensation.

PREPARATION TIME: *15 minutes*
COOKING TIME: *10 minutes*
SERVES 6

1 x 425 g can pineapple rings
in natural syrup
½ teaspoon ground cardamom
pinch ground cloves (optional)
⅓ cup reserved pineapple syrup
2 tablespoons Bourbon whiskey
or brandy
2 tablespoons brown sugar
⅔ cup thickened cream, whipped

1 Drain the pineapple rings and reserve the juice. Place the pineapple rings in a heat resistant baking tray. Combine the cardamom, cloves, pineapple syrup and whiskey. Pour over the pineapple rings. Sprinkle with brown sugar.
2 Preheat the barbecue, place the tray directly on the grill and cook for 10 minutes, turning once during cooking. Serve with lightly whipped cream.

Vanilla Bananas

A classic recipe with a difference. The hickory smoke flavour tempts the taste buds – your guests will want seconds. Best cooked on a kettle barbecue.

PREPARATION TIME: *10 minutes*
COOKING TIME: *12 minutes*
SERVES 6

6 soaked hickory chips
(optional)

6 bananas, peeled and
thickly sliced
2 tablespoons lime juice
2 tablespoons water
1 teaspoon vanilla
essence
¼ cup golden syrup
⅔ cup sour cream, to serve

Hula Hula

1 Preheat kettle barbecue, then add the soaked hickory chips, if using. Cover the barbecue and allow to smoke.
2 Place banana slices in a heat-resistant baking tray. Blend all other ingredients and pour over the bananas.
3 Set the tray directly on the barbecue grill, cover the kettle and cook for 12 minutes.
4 Serve the bananas on individual plates with the remaining syrup and a dollop of sour cream.
Note: Hickory wood chips are soaked well, then added to a preheated kettle barbecue before putting in the food. These chips create an aromatic hickory smoke which imparts a distinctive taste to the food being cooked.
Serve a selection of tropical and other fresh fruits on a bed of crushed ice for a stunning conclusion to your barbecue. Mango wedges, pineapple slices, bananas and pawpaws look great. Add other available fruits for variety in colour.

Pears with Ginger Custard

Pears are a superb fruit to use in this exquisitely subtle dessert.

PREPARATION TIME: *25 minutes*
COOKING TIME: *10 minutes*
SERVES 6-8

6 pears
¼ cup bottled preserved ginger pieces in syrup
3 tablespoons sultanas

GINGER CUSTARD
2 cups milk
2 tablespoons preserved ginger syrup
½ cup sugar
3 egg yolks
¾ cup cream

1 Using an apple corer, scoop out the centre of each pear to remove the core and leave a small hollow. Cut each pear in half. Drain the ginger and reserve the syrup. Finely chop and combine the ginger and sultanas. Place a small amount of filling into the hollow of each fruit and wrap in heavy-duty foil. Set aside until required.
2 To make Custard: Heat the milk, ginger syrup and half the sugar, stirring until sugar dissolves. Whisk the yolks with remaining sugar until thick and light. Add a little of the hot milk and mix well. Return the egg and milk mixture to the pan. Stir over a low heat until the custard thickens. Add the cream and cover pan until serving.
3 Cook pears on a preheated moderate barbecue grill for 10-15 minutes or until tender. Serve with warm Ginger Custard.

Orange Le Hot

This unique, refreshing flavour combination is a must for you to try.

PREPARATION TIME: *15 minutes*
COOKING TIME: *15 minutes*
SERVES 6

6 navel oranges

¼ cup Grand Marnier
2 tablespoons lime juice
3 dashes Tabasco or chilli sauce
2 tablespoons water
¼ cup brown sugar
orange rind
mint leaves

1 Cut the oranges just through the skin around the middle. Remove the skin from the top of the oranges with a grapefruit knife. Cut a cone-shaped section from the top of each orange to create a small hollow. Place oranges, hollow upwards, in a heat-resistant baking tray.
2 Combine Grand Marnier, lime juice, Tabasco sauce, water and brown sugar in a small bowl. Spoon the sauce into the hollows of the oranges, soaking them well. Cover the dish with a double layer of heavy-duty or industrial-strength foil.
3 Preheat the barbecue. Place the tray directly on the grill and cook the oranges for 15 minutes. Garnish with mint and orange rind. Serve with almond bread if desired.

Bananas Jamaica

If fresh limes are not available, use lemon juice for this recipe.

PREPARATION TIME: *10 minutes*
COOKING TIME: *10 minutes*
SERVES 6

1 tablespoon lime juice
30 g butter, melted
¼ cup rum
6 bananas, peeled and halved lengthways
3 tablespoons brown sugar
vanilla ice-cream, to serve

1 In a heavy-duty, heat-resistant baking tray, stir together lime juice, butter and rum. Add the bananas to the tray and turn to coat. Sprinkle with brown sugar.
2 Preheat barbecue grill, place the flat tray directly on the grill and cook for 10 minutes or until bananas are soft. Spoon onto individual plates and serve with good-quality vanilla ice-cream.

Rather than serving dessert at your barbecue, serve a selection of homemade biscuits and slices. Often people don't feel like dessert, just something sweet to have with coffee.

Pineapple and Coconut Tart
Place a can of undrained, crushed pineapple into a small pan. Dissolve 1 tablespoon custard powder in 3 tablespoons milk. Add to the canned pineapple and stir over a low heat until it thickens. Allow to cool. Spread in the base of a ready made 20 cm pastry case. Whip 300 mL cream, sweeten to taste with icing sugar and add ¼ teaspoon vanilla essence. Spread over the top of the pineapple and sprinkle with toasted shredded coconut.

Above: Pears with Ginger Custard. Below: Orange Le Hot

Mandarins with Ginger

This is a quick and easy dessert and lends itself well to the conclusion of Asian in-spired barbecue meals.

PREPARATION TIME: *10 minutes*
COOKING TIME: *10 minutes*
SERVES 6

2 x 175 g cans mandarin segments
½ cup sugar
¾ cup syrup from the can
2 tablespoons finely chopped glacé ginger
1 teaspoon grated orange rind

Mandarins with Ginger

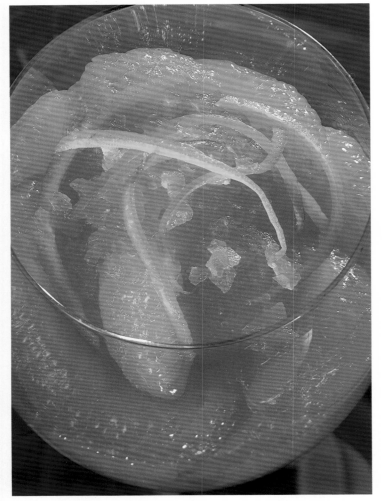

1 Drain mandarin segments and divide between six small foil containers or small individual heat resistant dishes.
2 Combine sugar, syrup, ginger and orange rind in a pan and stir over a low heat until sugar dissolves. Simmer for 5 minutes. Cool slightly and pour over the mandarin segments. Cover each with foil and place in a baking tray. Set aside to serving time.
3 Place on a moderate barbecue grill and cook until the syrup is boiling. Serve the Mandarins with Ginger immediately.

Baked Sweet Potatoes with Spiced Cream

This robust vegetable allows itself to blend wonderfully with Spiced Cream.

PREPARATION TIME: *15 minutes*
COOKING TIME: *15-20 minutes*
SERVES 6

2-3 medium size orange
sweet potato
30 g butter, softened

SPICED CREAM
⅓ cup thickened cream
1 tablespoon brown sugar
1 tablespoon maple syrup
or 2 teaspoons vanilla
essence
½ teaspoon ground cardamom
½ teaspoon ground nutmeg or mace
½ teaspoon ground ginger
¼ teaspoon ground allspice

1 Peel sweet potatoes and cut into 5 mm slices. Divide into six equal portions and place each in a double layer of heavy duty foil. Add a teaspoon of butter to each par-cel and wrap securely.
2 Place on coolest part of barbecue and cook for 15-20 minutes or until potato slices are tender. If the heat is too intense, they'll burn.
3 To make Spiced Cream: While the par-cels are cooking, combine remaining in-gredients and whisk with a fork until thick. When parcels are cooked, serve with a couple of dollops of Spiced Cream. Serve immediatly with fresh strawberries and sweet biscuits if desired.

Above: Baked Sweet Potatoes with Spiced Cream. Below: Bananas Jamaica (page 102)

Ice-cream Loaf

Soften 1 L vanilla ice-cream and 1 L strawberry ice-cream in the refrigerator. Whip 1 cup thickened cream and fold half into each of the ice-creams. Fold ¼ cup strawberry jam into the strawberry ice-cream. Spoon into a lined loaf pan 25 x 15 x 5.5 cm, in two separate layers. Refreeze until firm. Serve sliced with a jug of strawberry purée.

Strawberry Cheesecake

Strawberry Cheesecake

This lovely cheesecake can be made ahead of time and is perfect for large barbecue parties. It's ideal to transport to another location if entertaining away from home.

PREPARATION TIME: *20 minutes*
REFRIGERATION TIME: *4 hours*
SERVES *10-12*

200 g plain chocolate biscuits
60 g butter, melted
2 x 85g packets strawberry jelly crystals
2 teaspoons gelatine
1½ cups boiling water
2 x 250 g packets cream cheese
¾ cup cream, whipped

TOPPING
extra whipped cream
strawberries
chocolate curls

1 Crush biscuits in food processor or in a plastic bag with a rolling pin. Combine crushed biscuits and melted butter. Press into the bottom of a greased and lined 20 cm springform tin. Refrigerate while preparing the filling.
2 Place jelly crystals and gelatine in a bowl, add boiling water and stir until the crystals dissolve. Chill until partially set. Beat cream cheese until soft and gradually beat in partially set jelly. Fold through whipped cream and spoon into the prepared springform tin. Refrigerate until set. Carefully remove from tin, place on serving plate.
3 Decorate top of cheesecake with extra whipped cream, strawberries and chocolate curls.
Note: To make Chocolate Curls: Scrape strips of chocolate from the side of a block, use a vegetable peeler. Or melt 250 g chocolate, pour onto Laminex board. Allow chocolate to set to room temperature. Use a flat bladed knife to make curls. Hold the blade at an angle. Apply constant pressure to the blade with both hands. Pull the knife towards you. Varying pressure on the blade will alter the thickness of curl.

Fruit Kebabs

Fruit Kebabs

Just when you think you've tried every fruit recipe – here is a delicious new one.

PREPARATION TIME: *25 minutes*
COOKING TIME: *10 minutes*
SERVES 6

1 small pineapple
2 apples
2 bananas
1 tablespoon lemon juice
1 x 425 g can apricot halves, drained
1 x 250 g punnet strawberries, washed and hulled
¼ cup honey
60 g butter, melted
¼ teaspoon mixed spice

1 Peel the pineapple and cut into thick slices. Remove the hard core from the centre of each slice and cut each of the slices into six wedges.
2 Peel the apples and cut into quarters. Peel bananas and cut into thick slices. Place in a bowl and sprinkle with the lemon juice.
3 Thread pineapple, apples, bananas, apricot halves and strawberries alternately onto skewers. Combine honey, melted butter and mixed spice.
4 When ready to serve, grill over a preheated barbecue grill until lightly browned, brushing with honey butter mixture at regular intervals. Serve warm with whipped cream.
Note: To test if your pineapple is ripe, the centre spiky leaf should easily come free, when gently pulled. Any combination of seasonal fruit can be used. Choose ripe yet firm pieces of fruit.

Fruit Fool
Fold equal quantities of puréed fruit and whipped cream together. Sweeten to taste with icing sugar and serve in tall glasses. Garnish with fresh fruit or mint leaves.

USEFUL INFORMATION

Recipes are all thoroughly tested, using standard metric measuring cups and spoons. All cup and spoon measurements are level. We have used eggs with an average weight of 55 g each in all recipes.

CUP & SPOON MEASURES

A basic metric cup set consists of 1 cup, ½ cup, ⅓ cup, and ¼ cup sizes. The basic spoon set comprises 1 tablespoon, 1 teaspoon, ½ teaspoon and ¼ teaspoon.

1 cup	250mL/8 fl oz
½ cup	125 mL/4 fl oz
⅓ cup	80 mL/ 2½ fl oz (4 tablespoons)
¼ cup	60 mL/ 2 fl oz (3 tablespoons)
1 tablespoon	20 mL
1 teaspoon	5 mL
½ teaspoon	2.5 mL
¼ teaspoon	1.25 mL

DRY MEASURES

Metric	Imperial
15 g	½ oz
30 g	1 oz
45 g	1½ oz
60 g	2 oz
75 g	2 ½ oz
90 g	3 oz
100 g	3½ oz
125 g	4 oz
155 g	5 oz
170 g	5½ oz
200 g	6½ oz
220 g	7 oz
250 g	8 oz

OVEN TEMPERATURE CHART

	°C	°F	Gas Mark
very slow	120	250	½
slow	150	300	1-2
mod. slow	160	325	3
moderate	180	350	4
mod. hot	190	375	5-6
hot	200	400	6-7

LIQUIDS

Metric	Imperial
30 mL	1 fl oz
60 mL	2 fl oz
100 mL	3½ fl oz
125 mL	4 fl oz
155 mL	5 fl oz
170 mL	5½ fl oz
200 mL	6½ fl oz
220 mL	7 fl oz
250 mL	8 fl oz

THE PUBLISHER THANKS THE FOLLOWING FOR THEIR ASSISTANCE IN THE PHOTOGRAPHY FOR THIS BOOK:

BARBECUES OFFSHORE
FORE AND AFT MARINE
COUNTRY FLOORS
COUNTRY TRADER
GREGORY FORD ANTIQUES
IN MATERIAL
LIMOGES
SEASONS GALLERY
VILLEROY AND BOCH
SHAUNA ARONEY PALM
BEACH ARTWORKS

GLOSSARY

burghul = cracked wheat
capsicum = sweet pepper
cornflour = cornstarch
eggplant = aubergine
flour = use plain all purpose unless otherwise specified
snow pea = mangetout
spring onion = shallots
zucchini = courgettes

Published by Murdoch Books, a division of Murdoch Magazines Pty Ltd 213 Miller Street, North Sydney NSW 2060

Murdoch Books Food Editor: Jo Anne Calabria
Home Economists: Kerrie Ray, Donna Hay,
Designer: Annette Fitzgerald
Art Direction for Photography: Elaine Rushbrooke
Photography: Ray Joyce
Illustrations: Barbara Rodanska, Bruce Whately
Index: Michael Wyatt

Publisher: Anne Wilson
Publishing Manager: Mark Newman
Managing Editor: Sarah Murray
Production Manager: Catie Ziller
Marketing Manager: Mark Smith
National Sales Manager: Keith Watson

Cataloguing-in-Publication-Data
Barbecue cookbook
Includes index
ISBN 086411 256 4
1. Barbecue cookery. I. Title.
641.5784
First printed 1992
Printed by Toppan Printing Co. Ltd, Singapore
© Text: Reuben Solomon 1992
© Photography and illustrations:

Distributed in the UK by Australian Consolidated Press (UK) Ltd, 20 Galowhill Road, Brackmills, Northampton NN4 0EE Enquiries – 0604 7604 56

ACKNOWLEDGMENTS

To my wife Charmaine, whose expertise and enthusiasm are an inspiration.
To my daughters Nina and Debbie for their encouragement and support.
To Darlene, my secretary, without whose persistent prodding this book would still be in my head.
To all my family and friends who never once grumbled at yet another barbecue meal.

Above: Mango Chicken (page 50). Below: Garlic and Ginger Chicken (page 51).